# WHALES
# DOLPHINS & PORPOISES

THE LITTLE GUIDES

# WHALES
## DOLPHINS & PORPOISES

**CONSULTANT EDITOR**
Peter Gill

FOG CITY PRESS

Published by Fog City Press
814 Montgomery Street
San Francisco, CA 94133 USA
Reprinted in 2000 (three times), 2001

Chief Executive Officer: John Owen
President: Terry Newell
Publisher: Lynn Humphries
Managing Editor: Janine Flew
Art Director: Kylie Mulquin
Editorial Coordinator: Tracey Gibson
Production Manager: Martha Malic-Chavez
Business Manager: Emily Jahn
Vice President International Sales: Stuart Laurence

Project Editor: Robert Coupe
Designer: Lucy Bal
Consultant Editor: Peter Gill

A catalog record for this publication is available from
the Library of Congress, Washington, DC.

ISBN 1 875137 80 7

Color reproduction by Colourscan Co Pte Ltd
Printed by LeeFung-Asco Printers
Printed in China

A Weldon Owen Production

# CONTENTS

PART THREE

# WHALES AND PEOPLE

# PART ONE

# WHALES AND
# THEIR WORLD

# UNDERSTANDING WHALES

In the past, when people thought of whales, they often conjured up images of giant fish that dominated the open oceans. We now understand that whales are not fish at all—and nor are they all giants. Like humans, whales are mammals. Like humans, too, they often live in large communities and exhibit a great deal of complexity in their social organization. Whales vary widely in their habitats. As well as inhabiting all of the Earth's oceans, they are encountered in many of its estuaries, gulfs, inland seas, large rivers and shallow coastal bays. Some species of whales have adapted to the warm, muddy fresh water of equatorial rivers; others to the icy seas of polar regions.

# WHAT ARE CETACEANS?

Whales, dolphins and porpoises belong to a single group of marine mammals known as the cetaceans. Scientists have classified them as belonging to the Order Cetacea, one of the subdivisions of the Class Mammalia. More than 80 different species are currently recognized by whale experts, although as research progresses, new ones are still being discovered.

**Unique mammals** Like other mammals, whales are warm-blooded and give birth to live young. But unlike other mammals, most whales have lost all hair, as an adaptation to their aquatic environment. Cetaceans, along with dugongs and manatees, spend all their time in the water and do not haul themselves onto land or ice to rest or breed, as seals and otters do.

**Great variety** Whales, dolphins and porpoises share many features in common. Yet they come in an

### AGILE AND FRIENDLY
Like all members of the genus *Lagenorhynchus*—commonly known as "lag" dolphins—Pacific white-sided dolphins are noted for their exuberant acrobatics and sociable nature. Many of them, like the one in the foreground, have two-tone dorsal fins.

*Humpback whale*

impressive variety of shapes, sizes and colors, as well as living in many different marine and freshwater habitats. They have

also developed a bewildering variety of adaptations for survival in their underwater world.

**Size, color and shape** Whales range in size from several small dolphins and porpoises that grow to as little as 4 feet (1.2 m) long, to the gigantic blue whale, which can grow to a length of more than 98 feet (30 m). Some species are a relatively drab uniform gray or brown color, while others are brightly colored with a motley collection of spots and stripes. Several have striking black and white markings. Some are long and slender, others short and robust. Some

have tall, scythe-shaped dorsal fins; other species have much smaller, triangular fins. A few have no fins at all. There are even variations among individuals of the same species; between males and females, youngsters and adults, and among populations in different parts of the world.

**DISTINCTIVE MARKINGS**
The black and white coloration of orcas makes them easy to identify at sea. Humpbacks also have white pigmentation, though the amount of white varies between individuals and between different populations.

*Orca*

13

# DIVERSITY OF FORM AND SIZE

**The more than 80 species of cetaceans exhibit an astonishing diversity of sizes, shapes and color patterns, as well as of habits and lifestyles. The relative lack of gravity in their watery medium has allowed some species to become enormous, yet some are no larger than humans.**

**Differences, obvious and subtle** Many species of whales, such as orcas, narwhals and blue whales, are relatively easy to identify, even for non-experts. Others differ from one another only in subtle ways and can pose indentification problems for the most seasoned whale watchers. Size is an important indicator of many species, yet it can be notoriously difficult to estimate the size of a whale or a dolphin—or even of a boat—in a vast expanse of "empty" sea, unless it can be viewed at close quarters. Other factors that can be important in recognizing individual species include the body shape, the character and size of the dorsal and pectoral fins and, in many toothed whales, the presence or absence of a well-defined beak. A few species, including the bowhead whale (pictured opposite) have no dorsal fin, and this at least narrows the field when trying to identify these species. Identification of some species is made difficult by the fact that they are rare and infrequently seen.

**Differentiating the sexes** In general, males and females are not easily distinguishable, although baleen females are larger than the males. Among toothed whales the reverse is often the case. External differences in some species are evident only in the genital region. In a few species, however, there are obvious differences. The male narwhal's tusk is probably the most obvious example.

---

**BLUE WHALE**
Although it bears some resemblance to its close relatives—the fin, sei and Bryde's whales, all of them large—the blue whale's sheer size and bulk make it unmistakable. Blue whales are the largest living creatures on Earth.

---

*Gray whale*

*Beluga*

*Humpback whale*

*Bowhead whale*

*Sperm whale*

*Killer whale*

*Blue whale*

*Bottlenose whale*

**VARIATION AMONG WHALES**

The pictures on this page, which are drawn to scale, give some idea of the dramatic variation among cetaceans. An adult human would be dwarfed by all the whales shown here. Even the beluga, the smallest of them, is twice the length of an average adult human.

# WHALE EVOLUTION

**Mammals are mostly terrestrial animals with body forms and lifestyles that are familiar to us. Cetaceans, however, are less familiar because they are specialized for life in water. For this reason, cetacean origins have long been obscure. In recent decades new approaches have helped to establish and refine patterns of relationship that reveal hitherto poorly understood aspects of cetacean evolutionary history.**

**Mammalian origins** The fossil record suggests that cetaceans were already present well over 50 million years ago. They seem to have arisen from a family of hoofed land mammals, of which the dog-sized *Mesonyx* (pictured below left) is an example.

*Mesonyx*

### The shift to water

A comparison of living cetaceans and living land mammals hints at the changes that occurred in the move to water. Initially an otter or fur-seal habit was likely, with the limbs used to move in water. The tail was also used, with a vertical beat helping with propulsion. At some stage the end of the tail became flattened into flukes. Early whales were probably tied to the land to breed, but otherwise they seem to have adapted rapidly to aquatic life. Important changes probably included the ability to hear underwater and the development of nasal plugs.

### TIMELINE TREE

This diagram shows one interpretation of the evolution of cetaceans since their ancestors made the transition to living in an aquatic environment more than 55 million years ago. Some of the more important ancestral forms are shown. Several evolutionary lines became extinct.

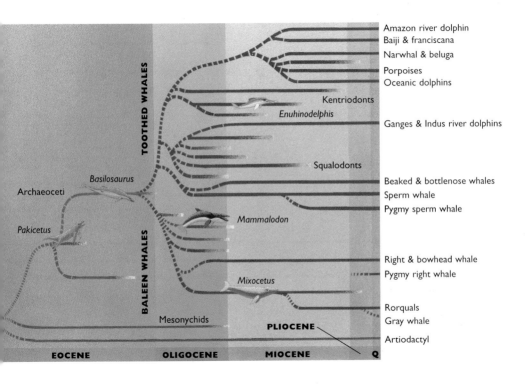

Amazon river dolphin
Baiji & franciscana
Narwhal & beluga
Porpoises
Oceanic dolphins

Kentriodonts

*Enuhinodelphis*

Ganges & Indus river dolphins

Squalodonts

Beaked & bottlenose whales
Sperm whale
Pygmy sperm whale

TOOTHED WHALES

*Basilosaurus*

Archaeoceti

*Pakicetus*

BALEEN WHALES

*Mammalodon*

Right & bowhead whale
Pygmy right whale

*Mixocetus*

Rorquals
Gray whale

Mesonychids

PLIOCENE

Artiodactyl

EOCENE    OLIGOCENE    MIOCENE    Q

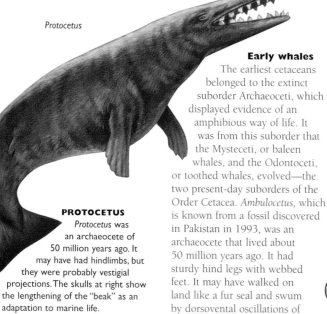

*Protocetus*

**PROTOCETUS**
*Protocetus* was an archaeocete of 50 million years ago. It may have had hindlimbs, but they were probably vestigial projections. The skulls at right show the lengthening of the "beak" as an adaptation to marine life.

### Early whales

The earliest cetaceans belonged to the extinct suborder Archaeoceti, which displayed evidence of an amphibious way of life. It was from this suborder that the Mysteceti, or baleen whales, and the Odontoceti, or toothed whales, evolved—the two present-day suborders of the Order Cetacea. *Ambulocetus,* which is known from a fossil discovered in Pakistan in 1993, was an archaeocete that lived about 50 million years ago. It had sturdy hind legs with webbed feet. It may have walked on land like a fur seal and swum by dorsovental oscillations of the spine. During this early stage of cetacean evolution, the climate was warm and stable, even in polar regions.

**Later developments** By about 38 million years ago, baleen whales and toothed whales had evolved, diverging from those archaeocetes that may have fed in warm, shallow coastal waters. From about 25 million years ago, the ancestors of both baleen and toothed whales became more diverse. By this time archaeocetes had become extinct, possibly as a

*Protocetus skull*

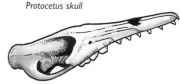

result of the rise of the toothed whales, which competed for the same food but had the advantage of echolocation.

**Geological changes** The evolution of modern cetacean lineages is linked with major geological changes in the Southern Hemisphere. The former huge southern supercontinent of Gondwana completed its fragmentation about 34 million years ago, when Australia and South America moved northward away from Antarctica. As a result of this, the polar climate cooled as Antarctica was left insulated

*Mesonyx skull*

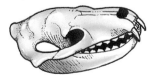

by the extensive circumpolar Southern Ocean. Perhaps the development of the new oceanic and climate patterns triggered the evolution of the two groups of cetaceans, with their new feeding patterns of filter feeding and echolocation-assisted predation.

**Early toothed whales**
Among the earliest toothed whales were two families: the squalodonts, or sharp-toothed dolphins, and the kentriodonts, the probable ancestors of living dolphins. Both families existed between about 25 million and 5 million years ago. Around 24 million years ago, sperm and beaked whales appeared. By this time there was already a significant diversity of species.

*200 million years ago*

*90 million years ago*

*Present*

**ON THE MOVE**
The breakup of Gondwana, which was completed about 34 million years ago, created opportunities for cetaceans to radiate.

# WHALE EVOLUTION continued

*Basilosaurus*

### ADVANCED ARCHAEOCETES

*Basilosaurus* and related archaeocetes lived from at least 34 to 40 million years ago. They formed an advanced archaeocete family, Basilosauridae, with cheek teeth and multiple pointed cusps and large sinuses in the skull base.

**Early baleen whales**
Modern baleen whales are huge toothless animals in which baleen plates hang from the upper jaw in a distinctively shaped skull. Tiny vestigial teeth in baleen whale embryos point, however, to a toothed ancestry. About 24 million years ago, one of the earliest ancestors of the baleen whales, *Mammalodon,* appeared. It was followed by the cetotheres, a family that had developed lobes of baleen for filter-feeding. These were probably similar to present-day rorquals,

but it seems likely that they were considerably smaller than modern rorquals.

**Climate change** A general climatic cooling occurred about 15 million years ago, and this led to an increase in polar sea ice. This triggered various oceanic changes around both poles that, in turn, initiated ecological changes which eventually produced the rich feeding waters that exist in the polar regions today. While their ancestors were small, the large size of most modern baleen whales

evolved in tandem with these changes. Their ability to store blubber helped with heat

### CLOSE RELATIONSHIP

Basilosaurid features such as cusped teeth and sinuses in the skull are also seen in early toothed and baleen whales, pointing to a close relationship between living cetaceans and basilosaurids. *Basilosaurus*, however, with its large body and strangely elongated vertebrae, was rather specialized and was possibly not directly ancestral to living forms.

*Mammalodon*

conservation in the cooler climate, and enabled long-distance migration. By about 7 million years ago, all of the present groups of cetaceans had more or less evolved into the forms that we recognize today.

**Evolutionary trends** Cetacean fossils are abundant on all the continents, and they are very diverse in form. By studying them, we can follow a number of evolutionary changes that occurred and led to the body form of today's cetaceans. To allow for efficient movement in water, the body gradually became more streamlined, shed hair and lost the hindlimbs. As well, the skull bones overlapped, and the neck become shorter and stiffer. The ear adapted to enable cetaceans to hear underwater, and the nostrils migrated to the top of the head to become blowholes. A thick, insulating layer of blubber developed, and changes that aided propulsion occurred in the tail, bone structure and muscles. Fins and flukes became modified to reduce drag and to facilitate steering control. One of the most significant developments was the divergence of the feeding apparatus, which led to the present division between baleen whales, which gulp large quantities of schooling prey, and toothed whales, which developed echolocation and teeth to catch single prey.

**TWO ANCESTORS**

The 16-foot (5 m) *Dorudon* of 25 million years ago was already taking on the streamlined appearance of modern dolphins. *Mammalodon*, which existed 23 million years ago in waters near southern Australia, was also probably streamlined, with well-developed pectoral fins and no sign of hindlimbs.

*Dorudon*

# TWO SUBORDERS

The key characteristics that separate the cetaceans into two suborders—baleen whales (Mysticeti) and toothed whales (Odontoceti)—are the presence or absence of baleen plates and teeth. Other differences include the shape of the skull, the appearance of the blowhole and the form of the ribs and the sternum.

**Contrasting skulls** When viewed from above, a toothed whale's skull is asymmetrical, perhaps because there is a single blowhole (the left nostril has developed at the expense of the right one). A baleen whale has a symmetrical skull and a double blowhole (although the apertures of the nostrils are unequal in size—the one on the left is usually slightly larger than the one on the right).

**Ribs and sternum** The ribs of whales vary greatly in numbers and structure, as well as in their attachment to the vertebral column and sternum. In most baleen whales the ribs have lost the head and articulate with their corresponding vertebra by means of the tubercle. The sternum is segmented in most toothed whales, but in baleen whales it always consists of a single bone.

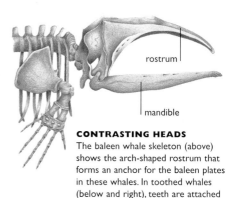

**CONTRASTING HEADS**
The baleen whale skeleton (above) shows the arch-shaped rostrum that forms an anchor for the baleen plates in these whales. In toothed whales (below and right), teeth are attached to the rostrum and mandible.

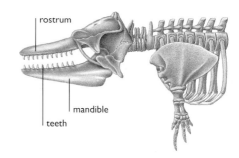

22

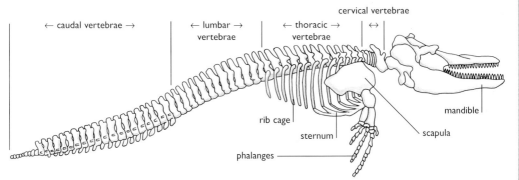

← caudal vertebrae →   ← lumbar → vertebrae   ← thoracic → vertebrae   cervical vertebrae ↔

rib cage
sternum
phalanges
mandible
scapula

**Size and speed** The most obvious difference between the two suborders is their relative size. Baleen whales are generally much bigger, although the smallest species are smaller than some toothed whales, such as the orca. Toothed whales are usually faster swimmers than baleen whales, since they must actively hunt their prey. Feeding for them is not simply a matter of swimming through a "soup" of food.

| Mysticeti | Odontoceti |
|---|---|
| Teeth lacking (except as embryonic vestiges) | Teeth present (although in some species they do not emerge through the gum) |
| Baleen plates present | No baleen plates |
| Skull symmetrical | Skull asymmetrical |
| External paired nasal opening | Single external nasal opening |
| One to three ribs have heads | Four to eight ribs have heads |
| Sternal ribs absent | Sternal ribs present |
| Sternum composed of a single bone, which articulates with the first pair of ribs | Sternum composed of three or more bones, which articulate with three or more pairs of the ribs |

# BALEEN WHALES

There are 11 species of baleen whales. These whales are filter feeders, using baleen (often called whalebone) to sieve out small planktonic organisms from the sea. They are also sometimes referred to as the "great whales"—an appropriate name for the larger members of this group.

**Plates of baleen** The most prominent feature distinguishing baleen from toothed whales is their baleen, horny plates hanging from their upper jaws. This baleen consists of a fibrous material similar to our fingernails.

**Huge and not so huge** The blue whale, the largest animal ever to have lived, grows more than 100 feet (30 m) long and weighs up to 180 tons (198 tonnes). The smallest baleen whale, the pygmy right whale, grows to more

### HUMPBACK ACROBATICS
Huge humpbacks can frequently be observed rolling over and over, often in the wake of boats, showing off the extensive whiteness of their bellies, flippers and flukes, their immense bodies set off by cascades of foam.

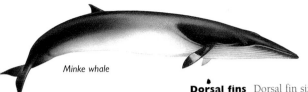
*Minke whale*

than 20 feet (6 m). Females are larger than males, perhaps to cope with the long fast required while bearing and feeding calves during their annual migrations.

**Long lifespans** Some baleen whales are thought to be more than 100 years old, so we may think of them as having lifespans roughly equivalent to those of humans. We can determine the age of dead baleen whales by examining cross-sections of the waxy plugs found in their ear canals. These form growth rings similar to the ones that form on trees—layers of shed skin alternate with layers of ear wax.

**Dorsal fins** Dorsal fin size and shape are often clues to species identification. The largest family of baleen whales, the rorquals, all have a true dorsal fin, as does the pygmy right whale. However, in the gray whale a series of bumps replaces the dorsal fin, while right whales have no dorsal fin at all.

**Skin protrusions** Humpbacks have a series of bumps, called tubercles, on the upper side of the snout. In young humpbacks, each tubercle may sprout a single hair. Right whales have callosities— white protrusions of hardened skin—around their heads. These are usually homes for barnacles and "whale lice," small crustaceans that feed on dead skin.

**COMPARING SIZES**
The pictures below show the relative sizes of five of the six rorqual whales. The other rorqual, the humpback, ranks in size between the sei whale and Bryde's whale. Even the smallest rorqual, the minke whale, can grow as long as 35 feet (10.5 m).

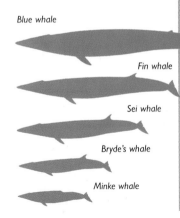

*Blue whale*

*Fin whale*

*Sei whale*

*Bryde's whale*

*Minke whale*

# BALEEN WHALES continued

**Food for baleens** It is curious that baleen whales, the largest animals in the sea, feed on some of the smallest. The zooplankton they eat are small oceanic animals: These are not to be confused with phytoplankton, the tiny plants on which the zooplankton feed. Making up the zooplankton are shrimp-like krill and other crustaceans, such as amphipods, copepods and free-swimming larvae of certain crabs. Zooplankton usually occur in schools or swarms, enabling the whales' baleen to capture large quantities of prey at one time. All whales are carnivores, but baleen whales are the marine equivalent of land-grazing animals, such as bison. Baleen whales may also eat schooling surface fish, such as herring, mackerel or pilchards, or such bottom fish as cod or sand lance. There are also records of baleen whales eating squid.

## BUBBLENETTING
Humpbacks in Alaska and Antarctica show an elaborate form of gulp feeding, called bubblenetting. The whale slowly rises from beneath a school of prey, expelling a circle of bubbles from its blowhole. These form a "net," causing prey to panic and converge. Whales then rise through the concentrated prey, with mouths wide open.

**Feeding techniques** Baleen whales eat as much as 3 to 4 percent of their body weight each day. These whales employ one of three basic methods of feeding: skim feeding, gulp feeding or bottom feeding.

**Skim feeding** Skim feeding is used by right whales, including the bowhead, and by the sei whale. With its mouth open, the whale swims slowly along near the water surface through a slick of zooplankton. Water flows into the mouth and strains out through the baleen in a continuous flow.

**Gulp feeding** Rorquals have a unique adaptation for feeding. Their throat pleats expand and increase the amount of food they can swallow. After expanding with each mouthful, the pleats contract and the tongue forces water out through the filtering baleen.

**Bottom feeding** Bottom feeding is the common feeding method of the gray whale. A whale leaves a plume of disturbed mud as it forages along the bottom for shellfish, crabs and worms. Humpbacks, too, have been observed feeding on the bottom, flushing out sand lance, which is a burrowing fish.

### A BOWHEAD'S HEAD
Bowhead whales live in cold Arctic and Antarctic waters. They are very rotund, and their huge heads contain the longest baleen of any whale. Each side of the jaw contains 250 to 350 plates, which grow between 10 and 13 feet (3–4 m) long. In rare cases they can reach up to 17 feet (5.2 m) long. Notice the distinctive "necklace" of black spots on the bowhead's chin.

*Bowhead whale*

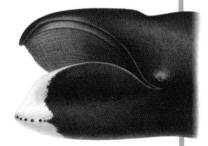

# BALEEN WHALES continued

**The right whales** Four species—the northern and southern right whales, the bowhead whale and the pygmy right whale—are collectively known as right whales. All four species have some feature in common: an arched rostrum; a bowed lower jaw, to accommodate very long, elastic baleen; certain skeletal characteristics; and a slow swimming speed. However, the pygmy right whale differs significantly from the other three and is classified in a family of its own. It is relatively small in comparison and has a small but prominent dorsal fin. The other right whales have no dorsal fin. Only northern and southern rights have callosities. Right whales differ in their distribution. Bowhead whales live only in Arctic waters, the northern and southern right

whales remain in their respective hemispheres, and the pygmy right lives only in temperate waters of the Southern Hemisphere.

**The gray whale** The single species of gray whale is a family of its own. Although naturally gray all over, it is usually blotched with patches of barnacles and whale lice. In form and size it falls between the "black" northern and southern right whales and the more graceful rorquals. Gray whales now live only in the North Pacific Ocean, where they migrate between the

**SMALL FIN**
The blue whale's sickle-shaped dorsal fin is distinctive for being extremely small and stubby—in marked contrast to the animal's huge overall size—and for its location three-quarters of the way along the back.

cool feeding grounds off Alaska and the warm lagoons of Baja California.

**The rorquals** The rorquals, with six species, make up the most diverse family of baleen whales. Five of them—the blue, fin, sei,

Bryde's and minke—make up the genus *Balaenoptera*. The humpback has a genus of its own, and in many ways differs from the other rorquals. The word rorqual derives from an old Norse word meaning "groove-throat." All six rorquals have a large number of throat pleats which allow the gullet to expand. All rorquals have dorsal fins, short baleen plates and heads that are flat on top, rather than arched or curved like those of other baleen whales. Body markings vary, from the dappled slate blue of the blue whale to the subtle swirling chevrons of the fin whale. Apart from Bryde's whale, which spends the year in warm seas, most of the rorquals are great migrants, traveling between tropical and polar waters. Early in the twentieth century rorquals were the mainstay of the whaling industry, particularly in the Antarctic. They were vulnerable to whaling because of their large populations and their tendency to assemble in huge groups in feeding and breeding areas.

**The humpback** The humpback is stockier than the other rorquals and is a much slower swimmer. Its most remarkable feature is its pectoral fins, which are about one-third as long as its body. Despite its slowness, this whale is very acrobatic. It has a remarkably long, complex song.

**TYPICAL RORQUAL**

With its characteristic narrow snout, its erect, curved-back dorsal fin and slender flippers, the sei whale looks like a typical rorqual. From a distance, it is easily confused with Bryde's and the fin whale.

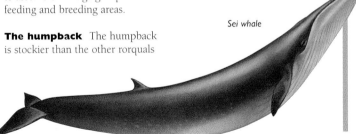

*Sei whale*

29

# TOOTHED WHALES

**The feature that unites all of the toothed whales is the possession of teeth. Toothed whales have perpetuated what was apparently the feeding mode employed by the earliest whales more than 45 million years ago: selecting and capturing individual prey.**

**Heads and mouths** The most obvious differences between toothed and baleen whales are in their heads and mouths. Toothed whales, for instance, have only one blowhole, whereas baleen whales have a pair. As we have seen, however, teeth are the principal distinguishing feature. Some oceanic dolphins have up to 260 cone-shaped teeth, evenly distributed between their upper and lower jaws. At the other end of the spectrum, the male narwhal

**GROUP TRAVEL**
Fraser's dolphins are tropical deep-water dolphins that often travel in groups of up to 500, and even sometimes 1,000 individuals. They sometimes also associate or feed with other species of tropical toothed whales and dolphins.

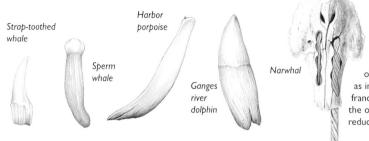

Strap-toothed whale

Sperm whale

Harbor porpoise

Ganges river dolphin

Narwhal

## TEETH VARIATION
The size, shape and number of toothed whales' teeth vary greatly from species to species. Sometimes there are scores of teeth in each side of the jaw, as in the common dolphin and the franciscana. Squid-eating species, on the other hand, often have greatly reduced numbers of teeth.

has only two teeth, both in its upper jaw, and one of these grows outward to form a spiral tusk.

**Size and body form** In size, toothed whales range from the tiny 5-foot (1.5 m) vaquita of the Gulf of California, to the 60-foot (18 m) sperm whale, one of the giants of the ocean. Like baleen whales, most toothed whales are streamlined in appearance, but their body shapes vary. Many, like the blunt-nosed sperm whale, are solid and bulky; others, including

the strap-toothed whale and most dolphins, are sleek and tapering. Most have a dorsal fin, but a few, such as the beluga, have only a raised hump. Beaked whales have a pair of throat grooves, but other toothed whales have no ventral feeding grooves.

**Feeding patterns** Some toothed whale species laze during the day, and at night hunt fish and squid that rise to the surface in darkness. Many dolphins hunt during the day, when schooling

fish cluster, and socialize at night. To capture prey, toothed whales use their excellent sight and hearing, as well as echolocation, a remarkable natural sonar system that is shared by all species. One aspect of toothed whales' behavior is their tendency to feed in groups, acting cooperatively in herding prey. Whales that feed close to shore do so in smaller groups than oceanic dolphins. A few species, however, seem to be solitary hunters.

31

# TOOTHED WHALES continued

**Sperm whales** At first glance there is a huge disparity in this group. The sperm whale, the largest toothed whale by far, grows to about 60 feet (18 m). The pygmy sperm reaches only 11 feet (3.4 m) and the dwarf sperm is a mere 9 feet (2.7 m) long, making it one of the smallest animals to be dignified with the term "whale."

## A PREY TO HUMANS

The sperm whale was extensively hunted during the last three centuries, because it produced the finest and most valuable oil—not from its blubber, but from spermaceti organs inside its vast head. Despite this, it is still relatively abundant.

All three species have a large melon (in male sperm whales a quarter of the body length), a short, narrow lower jaw tucked under the head and no functioning teeth in the upper jaw.

**The sperm whale** The sperm whale, or cachalot, is a most intriguing whale. Its distinctive blow slants forward at 45°, making it easy to distinguish at sea. It has a dorsal hump rather than a fin. It is found in all the oceans to the edge of the polar ice, and it feeds mainly on squid (in some areas on fish) along continental shelf edges, around oceanic islands, over seamounts and in areas of upwelling in deep water.

**Males and females** Sperm whales are unusual in that males grow to nearly twice as long and weigh up to three times as much as females. They also live largely separate lives. Females and very young animals remain in "nursery" schools in temperate to equatorial waters; young males live in "bachelor" schools in the same waters. In summer, mature males migrate to squid-rich polar waters, returning in winter to mate and socialize with the females. Sperm whales have a low reproductive rate, with females calving every four to six years. Female calves remain with their group for life.

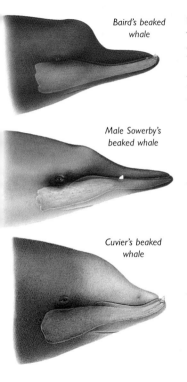

*Baird's beaked whale*

*Male Sowerby's beaked whale*

*Cuvier's beaked whale*

**Pygmy and dwarf sperm whales** Little is known of either of these species. Although they have definite dorsal fins, their small size, slow unobtrusive movements and indistinct blow make them difficult to sight at sea. Consequently, what we know about them comes mainly from strandings. Their diet consists mainly of squid and cuttlefish, fish and small crustaceans. Both species occur in temperate to tropical waters, where they apparently feed along the slopes of continental shelves, diving to at least 1,000 feet (300 m). Widely distributed in all major oceans, they strand occasionally, most notably off South Africa, Australia, and the southeastern United States. They are usually seen in groups of fewer than ten.

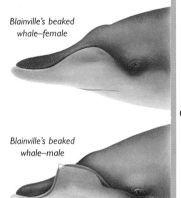

*Blainville's beaked whale–female*

*Blainville's beaked whale–male*

**BEAKED HEADS**
The general evolutionary trend in beaked whales has been toward a reduction in the number of teeth. The females of most species have no teeth at all, or at least their teeth remain invisible. In most males, there are no teeth in the upper jaw and just two to four teeth in the lower jaw which are often large and conspicuously visible.

33

# TOOTHED WHALES continued

**Beaked whales** The 20 or so identified species of beaked whales make up the least known group of cetaceans. All are small to medium-size deepwater species with unobtrusive habits that make them difficult to identify, let alone study. Their characteristic physical features are the lack of a central notch in the tail flukes, a single pair of throat grooves, a dorsal fin placed well back on the body and a lower jaw that extends to or past the upper jaw. Size varies from the 42-foot (12.8 m) Baird's beaked whale to the 11-foot (3.7 m) Peruvian beaked whale. Their apparent rarity may simply reflect their deep-sea habitat and their reclusive habits. Some species, such as the southern bottlenose and Arnoux's beaked whales, are relatively abundant. Others, however, are undoubtedly rare.

Beaked whales are all deep divers that feed mainly on squid. Some species may dive as deep as sperm whales do. They have many fewer teeth than other whales, a feature characteristic of a squid diet.

**SOUGHT-AFTER TUSK**
The narwhal's bizarre tusk has meant that this whale has been steadily hunted since the Middle Ages. Until the early seventeenth century, the tusk was sold for an exorbitant price as the horn of the legendary unicorn.

**PROTRUDING TEETH**
The two teeth in the lower jaw of the strap-toothed whale grow up and over the upper jaw. These teeth may be a sexual characteristic to help determine the fittest males for mating.

**Related species** Narwhals and belugas are two related species that are found only in Arctic and subarctic waters, where their lives are interwoven with the seasonal changes of the sea ice. Both species are found close to land, often in bays and fiords.

### Belugas

With its white skin, lack of a dorsal fin, flexible neck and expressive face, the beluga is one of the most distinctive of whales. Calves, born in spring and summer, are gray; some whales turn white by the age of five. They feed on a variety of prey, from bottom-dwelling mollusks to fish and zooplankton. They are preyed on by polar bears and orcas. There are five distinct populations throughout the Arctic and subarctic. Belugas follow the spring melt, congregating in large herds during the summer in estuaries and coastal waters.

### CONTRASTS

Its white color is one characteristic that distinguishes the adult beluga (above) from other whales. Another is its small, bulbous head and very short beak. In contrast the pygmy sperm whale (below) is dark bluish gray and has a distinctively rectangular-looking head and shark-like snout.

### Narwhals

Narwhals, which are smaller and more ice-adapted than belugas, rarely venture below the Arctic Circle. They prey on squid and on fish such as cod and halibut. Living in family groups of up to 20, narwhals aggregate and calve in midsummer while close inshore, and then follow the advancing ice edge out to sea when winter begins. They may winter in permanently open pools in the sea ice known as polynyas. Narwhals and belugas are often seen together.

35

# TOOTHED WHALES continued

**The dolphin family** The family Delphinidae, the oceanic dolphins and their relatives, contains 33 named species and is the most diverse of all cetacean families. However, the number of dolphin species is uncertain. For example, while bottlenose dolphins are currently recognized as one species worldwide, differences in size, color and habitat lead some scientists to believe that there may actually be two or three species. This group also includes orcas and their smaller relatives, and pilot whales.

**EASILY CONFUSED**
The Irrawaddy dolphin looks a little like a beluga and is thought by some researchers to be close to the beluga family. It is sometimes also confused with the finless porpoise.

**COMMON DOLPHIN**
The short-beaked common dolphin is one of the most acrobatic of dolphins. It is easily distinguished by the hourglass pattern on its side.

**A range of variation** Dolphins range in size from orcas, which grow to more than 30 feet (9.5 m) long, to the black dolphins of Chile, at a little more than 5 feet (1.6 m). Some, such as orcas, range worldwide; others, such as Hector's dolphin, which is found only around New Zealand, are

restricted. Many are deep-ocean species, while a few, such as the tucuxi of the Amazon and the Irrawaddy dolphin of Australasia, haunt tropical rivers and tidal mangrove areas. Some, such as Fraser's dolphin, are strictly tropical; others, such as the northern right whale dolphin (one of only two dolphin species to lack a dorsal fin), are found only in cool water.

**Living in groups** Social organization among dolphins is complex and highly structured. In many species, family groups stay together for life. Dolphins may form temporary groups of many thousands, apparently related to their feeding behavior. Cooperative behavior is very useful when herding prey, such as small schooling fish, or avoiding predators, such as sharks. In general, large concentrations of prey can attract large groups of animals. Many oceanic dolphins are nomads that roam the deep sea in large groups in search of schooling fish and squid. Coastal and estuarine dolphins, which have a more reliable food supply, form much smaller groups.

# TOOTHED WHALES continued

**Porpoises** There are only six species of porpoise. All are small, the largest being little more than 7 feet (2.1 m) long. The vaquita, at slightly less than 5 feet (1.4 m), is the smallest of all cetaceans. Porpoises typically have small flippers and no beak and, except for the finless porpoise, all have a dorsal fin. Unlike the conical teeth of dolphins, the teeth are flattened to cutting edges, which enables porpoises to slice their prey. Porpoises usually form smaller social groups than dolphins do.

**Distribution** For such a small group, porpoises are distributed very widely around the globe. Several are basically coastal in their habitats. The vaquita, which occurs only in the northern part of the Gulf of California, is the most restricted in its range. The harbor

**FRIENDLY WHALE**
The bottlenose dolphin is an oceanic species that frequently forms close associations with humans. Mature males often form very small groups of just two or three animals.

porpoise, on the other hand, is common along the North Atlantic and North Pacific coasts, where it bottom feeds in turbid water. Finless porpoises inhabit the warm, shallow coasts, estuaries and rivers of Asia. Burmeister's porpoise prefers the cooler waters of the coasts along the southern half of South America, being driven farther north on the Pacific coast by the cold Humboldt

Current. Dall's porpoise inhabits the cooler waters of the North Pacific, from Japan to California. The spectacled porpoise is distributed in the cool waters of the Southern Ocean, although it has rarely been sighted at sea. Strandings and a number of sightings suggest that it may have a circumpolar distribution.

**River dolphins** Several species of river dolphin are among the rarest and most threatened of cetaceans. They are generally regarded as the most primitive group of cetaceans and, as with many cetacean groups, their classification is still under debate.

**Special adaptations** All river dolphins show specialized riverine habitat adaptations: broad pectoral fins to aid maneuverability; and a mobile neck that allows them to move their heads from side to side, possibly for scanning with echolocation. The baiji and the franciscana each has a dorsal fin;

the other species have merely a dorsal ridge. All have small eyes. Some, such as the Ganges river dolphin, are functionally blind. They live in almost permanently muddy water and rely totally on echolocation to find prey.

### LITTLE-KNOWN PORPOISE
The spectacled porpoise is the least understood of porpoises. Only one or two at a time have ever been sighted, and almost nothing is known of its diet, biology and behavior.

**SEA-DWELLER**
Although it is classified as a river dolphin, the franciscana lives only in the sea and never ventures into rivers.

**Coasts and rivers** The franciscana occurs in nearshore waters along the Atlantic coast of South America, but the other river dolphins have colonized some of the greatest rivers—the Amazon, Ganges, Indus and Yangtze. They have apparently adapted to the cycles of flooding and drought that characterize these rivers.

# WHALE, DOLPHIN OR PORPOISE?

When scientists classify a number of living things into a group, they look for characteristics to show both that they are related to each other and are significantly different from members of other groups. For example, anatomical and biological structure are important considerations in classification, but what about more arbitrary criteria, such as size?

**Sizing up whales** Although all cetaceans are sufficiently similar, in broad terms, to be classified as whales, we generally reserve the term "whales" only for the largest of them—those at least 10 feet (3 m) long. We tend to use "dolphins" for cetaceans that are smaller than this, and "porpoises" for animals that are slightly smaller again. This system works well enough for baleen whales, which all grow to more than 20 feet

### DOLPHIN AND PORPOISE
The northern right whale dolphin (left) and the Dall's porpoise (above) do not differ greatly in size and they have a similar black and white coloration. But the bulky appearance of Dall's porpoise contrasts strikingly with the sleek and slender lines of the northern right whale dolphin.

**PORPOISING DOLPHINS**
Like most dolphins, these short-beaked common dolphins use this energy-efficient form of travel known as "porpoising," adding to the confusion between the terms "dolphin" and "porpoise."

(6 m), but it is not particularly reliable when we try to apply it to toothed whales.

**Classification muddle** We get some idea of how confusing these terms can be when we consider that among the oceanic dolphins and their relatives, some animals are referred to as whales and others as dolphins, and the names bear no relation to size. The melon-headed whale, for example, grows to only 9 feet (2.7 m) long, while the bottlenose dolphin can grow up to 12 feet (3.7 m). A number of other whales, such as the pygmy killer whale, are also smaller than some dolphins, and some porpoises outgrow several dolphin species. Perhaps the one saving grace in this classification muddle is that no porpoise is larger than any whale.

**Dolphin difficulties** A problem with the term dolphin is that it applies to two distinctly separate groups of animals: oceanic dolphins and river dolphins. In fact, oceanic dolphins are much more closely related to porpoises than they are to river dolphins. The differences between oceanic dolphins and porpoises are really relatively minor, and some people refer to all small cetaceans as "porpoises." Indeed, the lack of differences reflects the relatively small amount of evolutionary time since the ancestors of these two groups diverged.

**LONG OR SHORT?**
Until recently, the short-beaked (above) and long-beaked (below) common dolphin were considered to be a single species. The length of the beak is the main difference between them.

# ADAPTED TO LIFE UNDERWATER

In an underwater environment, animals live in a medium that is fundamentally different from that inhabited by land animals. Land-dwelling mammals have load-bearing limbs to support and move the body. Because cetaceans live in water, a buoyant medium, limbs are not needed for support or propulsion.

**PAIRED NOSTRILS**
Like all baleen whales, the huge blue whale has a pair of blowholes, or nostrils. These are located on the top of the head, with prominent fleshy mounds. The blue whale's blow can be taller and stronger than that of any other whale.

**Conserving heat** The thermal and vascular adaptations of cetaceans are quite distinctive. Like other mammals, cetaceans maintain a constant warm internal temperature. Blubber insulates against the chilling effects of water, and heat-conserving counter-current exchange systems reduce heat loss in blood circulating near the surface. Because of their body size and proportions, cetaceans have a problem getting rid of excess heat generated by exercise. Many species use countercurrent exchange systems in the flippers, dorsal fin and flukes to radiate or conserve excess heat.

**Salt balance** Land mammals need water to maintain the correct salt balance in the body. But, how do cetaceans deal with water and salt? Ingestion of salt during feeding, and from swallowed water, seems unavoidable, but

**DO WHALES SLEEP?**

Sleep for humans means reduced muscle activity and reduced consciousness. Blood pressure and breathing rate drop, and the eyes close. Cetaceans apparently don't sleep quite the same way. In aquariums, animals rest quietly near the surface with the blowhole exposed. Their breathing rate is slower than usual, but it still seems to be voluntary, pointing to a wakeful level of consciousness. Anecdotal evidence, however, points to some species as seeming to sleep soundly for long times at the surface.

we don't understand salt balance mechanisms well. Probably the complex cetacean kidney helps in the excretion of excess salt.

**Blowholes** We can breathe through either nose or mouth, but cetaceans breathe only through the blowhole (nostril). Cetaceans have effective structures to close the blowhole underwater. In baleen whales, the two blowholes are blocked by large nasal plugs. During breathing, the plugs are retracted by fast-acting muscles that originate on the upper jaw in front of the blowholes. The action is remarkably fast, occurring in the brief interval when the whale breaks the water. Toothed whales have a more complex blowhole, because the nasal passages are modified for sound generation. Two nasal plugs are still present, but they are buried far inside the

**SURFACE SLEEPER**

Sperm whales have been reported as "sleeping" for long periods at the surface, thus causing a hazard to shipping. Because they need to breathe in air, whales would drown if they slept, or rested, for too long underwater.

head, where they close off the more internal parts of the nasal passages. The single external blowhole is a feature unique to toothed whales. Their airway is independent of their mouth and throat, so that the processing of food and breathing are separate.

# ADAPTED TO LIFE UNDERWATER continued

### STREAMLINED RORQUALS

The sleek bodies of the sei whale (left) and the fin whale (below) mean that they are often confused when seen from a distance. Both have bodies that are adapted to swimming at speed. Sometimes dubbed the "greyhound of the sea," the fin whale can reach speeds of 20 miles (32 km) per hour.

**Maintaining buoyancy** In most mammals the center of buoyancy lies forward of the center of gravity, so that the animal floats with the head raised. Marine mammals, however, have a lifestyle that requires the head to be submerged except when breathing. Head and body orientation can be changed by ballasting (weight redistribution) or by hydro-dynamics (swimming movements). Ballasting can involve lightening some bones. Alternatively, additional dense bone can be deposited, for example, in the ribs. Ballasting seems to be linked with slow swimming speeds. For faster moving marine mammals, swimming movements maintain appropriate head and body posture. It has been argued that

## RECORD BREAKERS

Perfectly adapted to life underwater, whales, dolphins and porpoises are the record breakers of the animal kingdom. Here are a few examples:

**The blue whale is the largest animal on Earth.** The heaviest ever recorded was a female weighing 209 tons (212 tonnes), caught in the Southern Ocean in 1947. The longest was another female, also landed in the Southern Ocean, in 1909, measuring 110 feet 2 inches (33.5 m) from the tip of her snout to the end of her tail.

**The low-frequency pulses** made by blue whales and fin whales, when communicating with members of their own species across enormous stretches of ocean, have been measured at up to 188 decibels—the loudest sounds emitted by any living source.

**The longest and most complex songs** in the animal kingdom are sung by male humpback whales. Each song can last for half an hour or more and consists of several main components.

**The humpback whale** also undertakes the longest documented migration of any individual mammal (a record previously believed to be held by the gray whale). One humpback, for example, was observed at its feeding grounds near the Antarctic Peninsula and, less than five months later, was seen again at its breeding grounds off the coast of Colombia. The shortest swimming distance between these two locations is 5,176 miles (8,334 km).

**The sperm whale is believed to dive deeper** than any other mammal. The deepest known dive was 6,560 feet (2,000 m), recorded in 1991. It was made by a male sperm whale diving off the coast of Dominica, in the Caribbean. Indirect evidence suggests that sperm whales may be able to dive to depths of at least 10,000 feet (3,000 m). The record for the longest dive by any mammal is also held by the sperm whale; on 11 November 1983, biologists working in the southwest Caribbean listened to five sperm whales clicking underwater during a dive lasting an astonishing 2 hours 18 minutes.

the spermaceti in the forehead of the sperm whale helps to maintain buoyancy. It appears more likely, however, that the forehead has a function in sound transmission.

### TAIL FLUKES

In many cases, physical adaptations with a "primary" purpose have also come to have "secondary" uses. For example, although tail flukes evolved as means of efficient propulsion, they also often serve, as they do with the humpback, as weapons of defense and as instruments for stunning prey.

*Humpback whale tail*

# MAMMALS OR FISH?

**Cetaceans are fast-moving aquatic carnivores. They have streamlined and maneuverable bodies propelled by tails rather than limbs. Their many fish-like characteristics, which are overprinted on basic, underlying mammalian structures, are adaptations to life in water.**

### Mammal variations

Cetaceans have a body form that lacks the projecting body parts seen in most mammals. As well, the expressive "face" typical of land mammals is largely obscured by blubber. Most mammals have forward-facing nostrils, but blowholes in whales are on the top of their heads. Dimples on the sides of whales' heads mark the position of the ears, but there are no external flaps or lobes. Behind the head, forelimbs are fin-like, without visible elbows or fingers. Generally, there are only small bony limb remnants, hidden far inside the body, and there is no hint of legs.

### Fish-like characteristics

Adaptation to aquatic life is a trade-off; some mammalian features cannot be lost fully but must be retained in modified form. The genitals, for example, do not protrude, except in sexually active males, and there is no scrotum. But perhaps the most obvious fish-like features are the dorsal fins and tail flukes. These are both new structures created by evolution. Presumably the dorsal fin is a hydrodynamic feature used in swimming. But in some cetaceans, the dorsal fin is small, and in a few it is absent. It is not clear how this sort of variation affects swimming ability. Horizontal flukes are present at the tip of the tail. These are supported only in the midline by the hindmost tail vertebrae, and

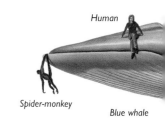

Human

Spider-monkey

Blue whale

46

## BIGGEST ON LAND OR SEA

The blue whale is the largest animal that has ever lived on Earth. Though it, and other cetaceans, have a number of characteristics in common with fish and reptiles, it is a warm-blooded mammal that has evolved bodily adaptations to a marine environment. Here we see the body shapes and sizes that different mammals have evolved to allow them to live in a wide range of terrestrial and aquatic environments.

otherwise are constructed of tough non-bony tissue.

### Swimming movements

Whales inherited their basic swimming movements from distant land-dwelling ancestors. Fast-moving land mammals flex the body up and down, in contrast to the side-to-side movements of many reptiles and amphibians. Cetaceans also flex the spine vertically, although they don't use fore- and hindlimbs for movement. Rather, powerful muscles above and below the vertebrae give rise to tendons that run back, via a narrow peduncle, to power tail flukes. Overall, propulsive muscles, tendons and vertebrae act to beat the flukes up and down, providing thrust. Most cetaceans can also bend the body sideways.

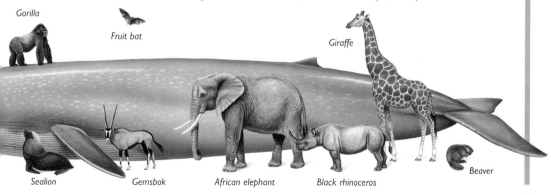

Gorilla

Fruit bat

Giraffe

Sealion

Gemsbok

African elephant

Black rhinoceros

Beaver

# DISTRIBUTION

Cetacean distribution is often related to surface water temperature and, for easy reference, the world can be divided into distinct temperature zones. But other factors are also important, from water depth to the proximity of land.

**Temperature zones** Polar waters are the high latitude zones around the Arctic and Antarctic. Moving toward the Equator from these waters, there are the subarctic and subantarctic zones, cold temperate, warm temperate, subtropical and, finally, tropical zones. Among the different habitats available within these zones are the coastal zone, the sublittoral zone (or continental shelf) and the pelagic (or offshore zone) over deep ocean basins.

**Baleen whale distribution**
Baleen whales are found in all oceans and, while some have fairly limited distributions, others occur worldwide. The bowhead whale, which is rarely found far from the cold Arctic icepack, has the most restricted natural distribution. The now remnant population of about 300 northern right whales is now restricted almost exclusively to

**SQUID EATER**
Deep-diving squid eaters, such as the sperm whale, prefer the edges of continental shelves, where upwelling occurs in deep water.

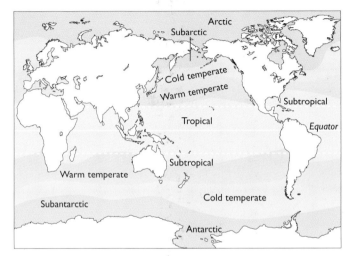

Arctic
Subarctic
Cold temperate
Warm temperate
Subtropical
Tropical
Equator
Subtropical
Warm temperate
Cold temperate
Subantarctic
Antarctic

**SURFACE WATER ZONES**
The distribution of many cetacean species follows a pattern closely related to water temperature. The different temperature zones are shown in this map.

and breed in Mexico, migrating between these areas. The minke and sei whales are both widely distributed, but the distribution of the sei is patchy and it does not occur as far north or south as does the minke. Fin and blue whales are also worldwide, but they prefer colder waters. Humpbacks are worldwide, but they divide their time between cold-water, high-latitude feeding grounds and warm-water, low-latitude breeding grounds. Bryde's whale occurs mainly in tropical, subtropical and some warm temperate waters throughout the world.

the western North Atlantic. The closely related southern right whale, however, is faring better; there are breeding populations of southern rights across the Southern Hemisphere. The pygmy right whale, too, seems to be fairly widely distributed in the temperate waters of the Southern Hemisphere. Gray whales are found mainly along the eastern North Pacific: They feed in Alaska

# DISTRIBUTION continued

### Worldwide toothed whales

A considerable number of toothed whales have a worldwide distribution, though some appear to have pockets of abundance and are absent from large areas within their overall range. Pygmy and dwarf sperm whales, for example, are both found in deep temperate, tropical and subtropical waters around the world, but there are vast areas where they have never been recorded. The sperm whale is more widely distributed, although it also has a patchy distribution:

Males frequently occur in polar waters, but females and calves have not been recorded there.

**Beaked whales** As a group, the beaked whales have a worldwide distribution, although few individual species are known in all oceans. The only species which appear to be truly worldwide

### LONG-RANGE MIGRANT
Each year gray whales make the 12,400-mile (20,000-km) round trip between Mexico and Alaska.

### DOLPHIN DISTRIBUTION
The map below shows the distribution throughout the world of the six species of oceanic dolphins belonging to the species *Lagenorhynchus*.

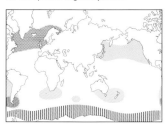

- ☐ Atlantic white-sided dolphin
- ☰ White-beaked dolphin
- ☐ Pacific white-sided dolphin
- ▨ Dusky dolphin
- ▥ Hourglass dolphin
- ▥ Peale's dolphin

- ☐ Vaquita
- ☐ Harbor porpoise
- ☐ Dall's porpoise
- ☐ Burmeister's porpoise
- ☐ Finless porpoise
- ☐ Spectacled porpoise

### PORPOISES

The map above shows the distribution of porpoises, members of the family Phocoenidae. All have restricted ranges, The harbor porpoise probably has the widest distribution, though it occurs only in the Northern Hemisphere.

are Blainville's beaked whale, which is probably the most widely distributed of any *Mesoplodon* species, and Cuvier's beaked whale, which is present in all except the polar waters in each hemisphere. But the distributions of even these whales appear to be patchy. Most other beaked whales seem to be restricted to one hemisphere and some occur only in fairly well-defined regions. Andrew's beaked whale, for example, is found only in cool temperate Australasian waters

**Blackfish** The six species that are commonly referred to as "blackfish"—the orca, the short- and long-finned pilot whales, the false killer, melon-headed and pygmy killer whales—are broadly worldwide in their distribution. However, only the orca is truly worldwide, and

even it is most common in polar waters. Interestingly, the closely related pilot whales have almost mutually exclusive distributions.

### NORTH PACIFIC WHALE

Baird's beaked whale (below), along with Stejneger's and Hubb's beaked whales, is restricted to the waters of the North Pacific Ocean.

# DISTRIBUTION continued

**Oceanic dolphins** Some of the "true" oceanic dolphins also have a worldwide distribution. The most widely distributed is probably the

bottlenose dolphin, which is found everywhere except in polar waters. Striped, rough-toothed and pantropical spotted dolphins are worldwide, though they are usually absent from cool temperate and polar waters. Common and Risso's dolphins live in temperate, tropical and subtropical waters worldwide, and the long-snouted spinner dolphin also inhabits tropical and subtropical waters.

**Living in icy waters** Like the bowhead whale, the narwhal and the beluga are predominantly

### RIVER DOLPHIN RANGES
The very limited distributions of the baiji, or Yangtze river dolphin (above), and the Amazon river dolphin (below) can be seen in these maps.

### DISTINCTIVE FIN
The tall dorsal fin of the male orca is often an identifying feature. This whale is found in all seas, from the Equator to the polar ice.

Arctic species, and both whales are circumpolar in their distribution. The beluga is most frequently observed in areas which are seasonally ice-covered, while the narwhal is found mainly in association with the pack ice.

**Restricted dolphins** Many of the "true" oceanic dolphins have a fairly restricted distribution. Some of their names—for example, the Pacific white-sided, the northern and southern right whale and the Atlantic white-sided and white-beaked dolphins—suggest the limitations of their distributions. The hourglass and dusky dolphins are solely Southern Hemisphere species, while the tucuxi occurs only near the coasts of southeastern Central America and northeastern South America.

**Very restricted species**
All four oceanic dolphins of the *Cephalorhynchus* species have very restricted ranges. Hector's dolphin, for example, occurs only in New Zealand coastal waters. The river dolphins, too, are restricted. One of them, the Indus river dolphin, is found only along a small stretch of the Indus River in Pakistan.

**Porpoises** No porpoise has a very broad range, and the small vaquita, which occurs only in the extreme northern end of the Gulf of California, probably has the most limited distribution of any marine cetacean.

**LARGEST OF THE DOLPHINS**
Despite their wide distribution in temperate, tropical and subtropical waters, Risso's dolphins, the largest animals that are called dolphins, have been little studied.

53

# ANATOMY
## AND
# SENSES

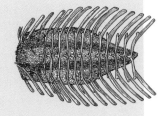

Cetaceans have been fully aquatic for more than 40 million years, and seem superbly adapted to life in water. But, upon close study, cetacean anatomy is seen to be full of compromise—there is no perfect anatomical design. Rather, the anatomy of whales and dolphins reflects a mix of factors: Some features have been inherited relatively unchanged from mammalian ancestors; some have evolved only relatively recently in response to the needs of aquatic life. As the early cetaceans moved into the sea, former aerially adapted senses had to quickly readapt to life underwater. And if a sense could not be modified to function effectively underwater, a new one had to be developed to replace it.

# WHALE ANATOMY

While in most mammals appendages such as ears and male genitals are external, in whales these have become internal to make for a streamlined body form, essential for easy movement through water. The layer of blubber beneath the skin is both an energy store and effective insulation.

**Mammalian heritage** Many cetacean features were inherited with little modification from distant ancestors, reflecting the warm-blooded and air-breathing active lifestyles of mammals. For example, whales have hair (albeit vestigial); a four-chambered heart supplying both lungs and body; and a diaphragm to aid breathing. Reproduction and parental care are complex: the genitals and anus are separate; young are nourished by a placenta in the uterus; and after birth the young are suckled by the mother. Body structures related to hearing and feeding show a distinctively mammalian form: There is a single lower jawbone on each side, and the ear contains three small auditory ossicles that transmit sound to the cochlea in a single periotic bone. The skull articulates at two condyles with the first of seven cervical, or neck, vertebrae, and the vertebrae of the trunk are separated into those with ribs (thoracics) or without (lumbar vertebrae). Anatomically, then, cetaceans are clearly mammals.

**TURNING WHITE**
Risso's dolphins are generally mid to dark gray, but as animals age the body color becomes lighter. Some older Risso's dolphins become almost white.

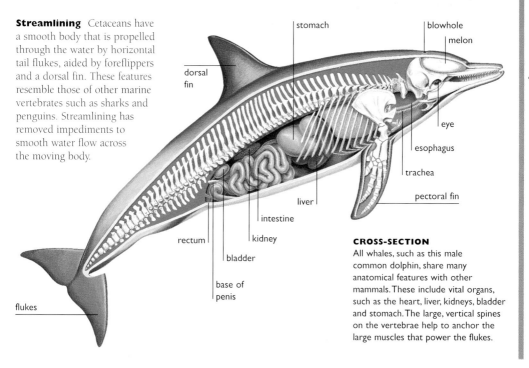

**Streamlining** Cetaceans have a smooth body that is propelled through the water by horizontal tail flukes, aided by foreflippers and a dorsal fin. These features resemble those of other marine vertebrates such as sharks and penguins. Streamlining has removed impediments to smooth water flow across the moving body.

stomach

blowhole

melon

dorsal fin

eye

esophagus

trachea

pectoral fin

liver

intestine

kidney

rectum

bladder

base of penis

flukes

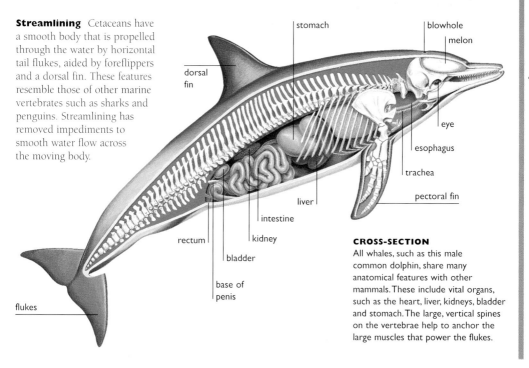

**CROSS-SECTION**
All whales, such as this male common dolphin, share many anatomical features with other mammals. These include vital organs, such as the heart, liver, kidneys, bladder and stomach. The large, vertical spines on the vertebrae help to anchor the large muscles that power the flukes.

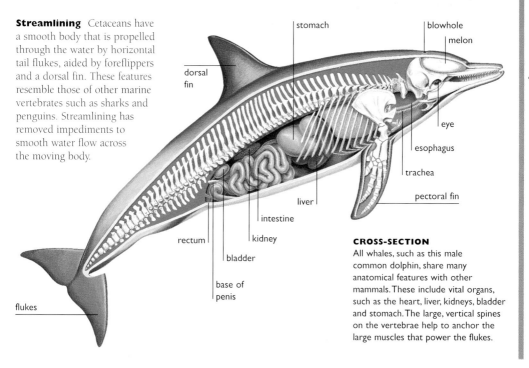

Anatomy and Senses

57

**Lost features** In adapting to aquatic life cetaceans have lost such characteristic mammalian external structures as significant body hair, sweat glands, an external ear lobe, a projecting nose and externally projecting genitals, scrotum and mammary glands. Remnants of the hindlimbs are internal, but very rarely a tiny vestigial leg occurs as an evolutionary throwback. Body outlines vary markedly, from slender, fast-swimming species to tubby slow swimmers with thick, heat-conserving blubber.

**Pectoral fins** All cetaceans have well-developed forelimbs, called flippers or pectoral fins, placed behind and below the head. The pectoral fins are stiff, without the movable elbow joint seen in most mammals, and there is little visible evidence of their internal structure. Yet these fins have the same basic internal form as a human arm, and presumably help in steering. Proportions vary greatly between species. In some, the fins are held rather rigidly out from the body, while in others, such as the humpback whale and the finless porpoise, they are quite mobile and may be used for slow-speed sculling. Internal variation involves the number of "fingers" (four or five digits); the number of phalanges—individual bones—in each digit; and the degree of splaying of the digits.

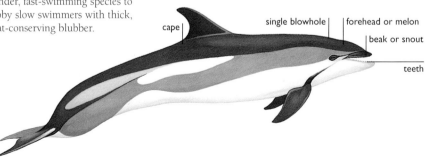

cape

single blowhole | forehead or melon

beak or snout

teeth

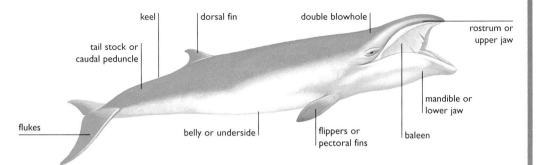

keel | dorsal fin | double blowhole

rostrum or upper jaw

tail stock or caudal peduncle

mandible or lower jaw

flukes

belly or underside | flippers or pectoral fins | baleen

**Dorsal fins** Most cetaceans have a prominent dorsal fin on their back, situated at or behind mid-length in most species. Some

---

**KEEPING WARM**

Cetaceans are large compared to most mammals, and therefore have a low surface-area-to-volume ratio. This ratio reduces heat loss, and, along with the layer of blubber, helps keep the animals warm.

---

whales, however, lack a dorsal fin, and in some species it is very attenuated. This fin is supported, not by skeleton, but by tough fibrous tissue inside it. Its size, shape and position vary, although it is not clear what this means in terms of controlling body orientation during swimming. It has been suggested that the dorsal fin also has a second role: that of regulating the temperature of reproductive organs.

**CETACEAN CONTRASTS**

Baleen whales, such as the pygmy right whale (above), and toothed whales, such as the Atlantic white-sided dolphin (far left), have basic mammalian features in common as well as other shared characteristics. However, as the diagrams show, they differ markedly in other important respects.

# WHALE ANATOMY continued

### HEAD RIDGES

Sei and other baleen whales have a single ridge on top of the head, extending from the tip of the beak to the blowhole. The Bryde's whale is unique in having a set of three parallel ridges on the top of the head.

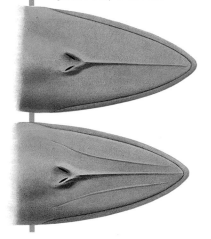

**Head and skull** The two groups of cetaceans—baleen and toothed whales—can be separated immediately based on the appearance of the head and skull. Differences between the groups reflect different feeding behaviors: baleen-assisted filter feeding in baleen whales and echolocation-assisted predation in toothed whales. In each group, the feeding method is closely linked with unique soft tissues and skull form. However, there are a number of common features. All cetaceans have a prominent upper jaw, or rostrum, which protrudes in front of the eyes. In bulbous-headed species, the rostrum cannot be seen externally, but is apparent on the skull. Under the skin, the head has a layer of blubber which prevents major muscles of the face reaching the surface and largely

### DEEP DIVER

Humpback whales usually lift their flukes before a deep dive. The patterns on the underside of these flukes have been used to identify thousands of individual humpbacks.

obscures the expressive face that is typical of land mammals. Most land mammals have forward-facing nostrils, but the equivalent in living cetaceans—the blowhole—is on top of the head.

**Eyes and ears**  Cetacean eyes are rather small and expressionless. They lie on the sides of the head, just behind the gape of the mouth. There are no eyebrows or lashes. Further back, behind and below the eyes, dimples or small holes on the sides of the head mark the position of the ears. There are no external ear flaps or lobes.

**Baleen whale heads**  A dominant feature of baleen whale heads is the large upper jaw, which carries a rack of baleen or "whalebone" on each side. Adult baleen whales do not have teeth, but multiple simple teeth occur in embryos. Baleen whales do not show the diversity of cranial structures shown in

**NETS AND BLUBBER**

Below left: One of the most intriguing features of whale anatomy is the existence of the large retia mirabilia ("wonderful nets")—massive structures composed of blood vessels beneath the backbone and ribs.

Below right: Forming a layer up to 20 inches (50 cm) thick, the dense blubber that lies beneath a whale's skin insulates the body against the chill of water and helps prevent heat loss.

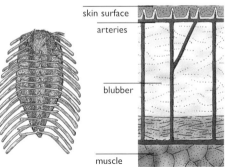

skin surface

arteries

blubber

muscle

toothed whales. Species differ most obviously from one another in the proportions of the upper jaw and in the shape, color and number of baleen plates. In slow-swimming right whales, long and narrow baleen arises from a narrow, high-arched upper jaw. The lower lips curve up to meet the arched upper jaw, covering the baleen. Rorquals have rather short baleen and a flat upper jaw. These gulp feeders drop the lower jaw far open to engulf huge mouthfuls of water and food. Baleen whales have widely separated lower jaws, which are toothless and lack baleen. They typically bow outward, and at the front they are not fused together, but are attached to each other by means of ligaments.

# WHALE ANATOMY continued

### Toothed whale heads

Externally, toothed whales show more variation in cranial structure than do baleen whales. Generally, the jaws are narrow and toothed; there is a bulbous "melon" that is associated with facial muscles and nasal sacs above the eyes and upper jaw; and a single blowhole opens high on the elevated forehead. Variations may include a bulbous forehead which obscures the jaws; broad and short rather than long and narrow jaws; a tooth complement that varies from hundreds to none (in most female beaked whales); and an anterior blowhole (in sperm whales).

### Transmitting sounds

A number of skull features in toothed whales probably help to produce and receive echolocation sounds. For example, the reduced

cheekbone presumably isolates the sound-producing front from the sound-receiving back of the skull. In each ear, the middle ear cavity is expanded into a complex sinus on the skull base. Bones in the inner ear are surrounded by air-filled foam that reflects sound and enables detection of the direction

### HUGE APPENDAGES

The pectoral fins of a humpback whale seem greatly out of proportion to the size of its body. At up to 16 feet (5 m) long, they are the longest appendages of any animal. Humpbacks often slap these huge fins heavily onto the water surface, an activity that may have many different functions.

of a sound source. The periotic—the earbone with the organs of hearing and balance—is loose in the skull, probably to eliminate spurious transmission of sound through the adjacent skull bones. The external ear canal is vestigial. Sound probably travels through the pan bone, in the lower jaw, and then through a fatty channel to the ear.

**Behind the head** The cetacean postcranial skeleton also differs from that of land mammals. The cervical vertebrae are foreshortened and may be partly or wholly fused. The form of the ribs in the thorax reflects aquatic life—the body is buoyed by water, without the need for the body support required by land animals. Thoracic structure will not support the weight of the body on land, which is why cetaceans often die when they strand. In all cetaceans,

lumbar vertebrae pass into caudal or tail vertebrae without a distinct pelvis. Only a remnant of the pelvic girdle remains, suspended below the spine.

**Whales' brains** Generally, the brains of cetaceans are large compared to their body size.

In many species the cerebral hemispheres are large and folded, with a well-developed outer layer. Blood supply to the brain is not by the normal mammalian route of the carotid arteries, but by way of blood vessels associated with the spinal cord.

**Other organs** Cetacean stomachs are chambered, usually with a large fore-stomach followed by a main stomach and smaller duodenum. Whales lack a gall bladder and appendix, and the liver is not lobed. The lungs, which lie near the heart, are supplied by a short, and often wide, trachea. The kidneys are large with many separate lobes—each effectively a small kidney in itself.

### KEEPING COOL

Whales need to shed the heat they generate during movement, but they must retain enough heat to maintain a stable temperature. They do this with the aid of countercurrent heat-exchange systems. Blood vessels carry blood from the cool outer shell to the warm body core. These are interlaced with vessels going in the opposite direction. If an animal overheats, warm blood is flushed to the fins, flukes and skin, and from here it dissipates into the water, while cooler blood flows to the body core.

# WHALES' SENSORY WORLD

Cetaceans evolved from land mammals. We can assume that their ancestors had the same five senses that we have—sight, touch, taste, smell and hearing—and that these senses were adapted, as they were in other land mammals, to receive messages through the medium of air rather than water. In their marine environment, whales still have these senses.

**Sight** Scientists used to think that cetaceans had poor eyesight, but for most species they have been proved wrong. The cetacean eye is well adapted to low-light conditions and can tolerate a great range of light intensity, from bright daylight to the extreme gloom of deep water. Some river dolphins, however, have almost dispensed with sight, though they can still distinguish between light and dark. Whales use sight to examine

**ADAPTABLE EYES**

A humpback's eyes are mobile and well adapted to life in the sea. At depth the pupils become very large, enabling the eyes to make maximum use of the low-light intensity; at the surface they are reduced to narrow slits. It is probable, though, that these whales have only a rudimentary sense of smell in the air.

## COLOR VISION

There is reason to believe that some dolphins have color vision. Although water is usually a semi-opaque medium that quickly filters out colors other than green and blue, the sometimes colorful markings on many cetaceans suggest that these species can recognize them at close quarters. Studies of dolphins have found that some show a preference for red and yellow objects. This suggests that at least some can discriminate between colors.

## WHITE CANARY

Belugas are sometimes called "sea canaries" because of their large vocal repertoire of clicks, yelps, squeals and whistles. This "music" is often audible to humans through the hulls of boats, and is, presumably, equally audible to other belugas.

their immediate environment, to look at objects of interest and to capture prey at close range. Sight may be particularly important for baleen whales, which lack the ability to echolocate. It is probably also invaluable in helping them to avoid predators.

**Eyes wide set** Many whales—including large species such as southern right whales—have their eyes set at the widest part of their head, and appear to have binocular vision. This means that their eyes, like those of humans, work together to focus on objects. Sperm whales, which have a huge head and their eyes set well back, probably have only monocular vision in each eye. The bottlenose dolphin, which has excellent binocular vision, also has the unique ability to move each eye independently of the other.

**Seeing in the dark** The extent to which whales use their eyes at great depths in the ocean is not known. Below about 650 feet (200 m), light levels are very low, but many species of toothed whales regularly dive and feed well below these depths. Many of the deep-sea animals they catch have light organs. Perhaps these whales have eyes adapted to detect the light emanating from these organs.

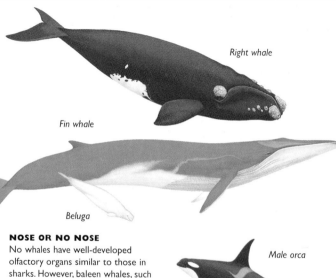

Right whale

Fin whale

Beluga

Male orca

### NOSE OR NO NOSE
No whales have well-developed olfactory organs similar to those in sharks. However, baleen whales, such as the right and fin whales, do have olfactory sensors that may allow them to smell at the surface. Toothed whales, such as the beluga and orca, have no olfactory organs.

**Smell** For land mammals, both taste and smell are important for detecting chemical stimuli. The structures that enable land mammals to detect smells do not operate in water, although fish, especially sharks, do have external receptors that allow them to sense chemicals carried through the water. Baleen whales do have olfactory nerves, but these are unlikely to operate at all underwater. They may, however, come into limited play at the surface, allowing the whales to "sniff the winds" in search of plankton-rich waters. Toothed whales have no olfactory equipment at all.

**Taste** All cetaceans do seem to use taste to some extent. It is obvious that some dolphins can distinguish between the tastes of different fish species. They have also been shown to be able to distinguish between what we would describe as sweet, sour, bitter and salty tastes. What seem to be taste buds are present on the tongues of several species of toothed whales. Some species have a small sensory organ, known as Jacobson's organ, which occurs at the front of the mouth and may further broaden tasting abilities.

**Using taste** Cetaceans may use taste in various ways. They may use it to investigate likely food items for signs of decomposition. Some researchers, for example, have tried, without success, to feed wild dolphins on dead fish. Dolphins also seem able to taste traces of other dolphins' urine or feces, allowing them to follow a "taste trail" where other dolphins have recently passed. Taste, too, is probably a means of sexual communication for dolphins. Bottlenose dolphins appear to "sniff" the genital area of females to find out if they are in estrus.

### PERFORMERS
Pacific white-sided dolphins are favorite acrobatic performers for whale watchers in the North Pacific Ocean. They clearly put their senses of sight and hearing to good use in their responses to the stimuli provided by human observers.

**Touch** A newborn cetacean calf's first sensations are probably the shock of entering the water, and then the first touch of its mother's skin as she nudges it to the surface to take its first breath. In the next few months, frequent physical contact will reinforce the bond between mother and calf. In most species touch remains an important lifelong means of social communication. Even very large right whales touch each other quite gently as a form of social contact; some other species, such as humpback whales, appear to communicate more by sound than by touch.

**Sensual touching** Courting whales often nibble or caress each other gently, but they may also resort to forceful physical contact and rough behavior, such as raking each other with their teeth. Gregarious social species, such as dolphins and orcas, maintain physical contact within their groups, even while swimming at high speeds. At well-frequented beaches in British Columbia in Canada, orcas appear to derive great pleasure from rubbing off flaking skin on the pebbly bottom. This kind of sensory stimulation is sometimes sexual in nature. For example, a male bottlenose dolphin may use its penis to explore objects, or a whale might rub its body against an inflatable boat that is similar in texture to a whale's skin. Touch may also have more routine applications, such as sensing the correct moment to open the blowhole when surfacing, or sensing disturbances to laminar flow while swimming.

**LAMINAR FLOW**
An important function of whales' skin is probably to help them swim more efficiently. Cetaceans need to achieve "laminar flow" of water over the body if they are to swim efficiently at high speed. If turbulence develops anywhere on the body surface, the laminar flow is interrupted. Hence the animal's body shape needs to be adjusted constantly while it is swimming. Many species of whales and dolphins appear to be able to do this, and it is thought that they manage it by using their highly sensitive skin as a pressure sensor. By monitoring the entire body surface for pressure or stretching points as it swims, the animal can continually keep its body in the correct shape for laminar flow to occur.

**Sound and hearing** In a dense medium such as water, sound travels four times as fast, and very much farther, than it does in air. The ear canal of a baleen whale is blocked by a waxy plug, which may transmit sound to the inner ear. In toothed whales, the ear canal is open, but we cannot be certain whether these whales hear through this canal, through the bones of the skull or through the fatty deposits in the lower jaw. All whales and dolphins seem to have excellent hearing. They can not only hear distant sounds, but also recognize the direction from which they come. Cetacean ear bones are surrounded by air-filled foam that reflects sound, and this enables a whale to detect the difference between the strength of the sound in each ear. This is only one of the many complex adaptations within the cetacean ear that indicate how important the sense of hearing is.

**Extra sense** Another sense, which it is possible that whales possess, allows some animals, such as many birds and sea turtles, to detect perturbations in the Earth's magnetic field. Crystals of the magnetic mineral magnetite have been found in a number of toothed whales, as well as in one humpback whale.

**HEARING**
While taste and touch mainly provide information about what is nearby, hearing is probably the most important of all the senses, because it can also convey information from a distance. Singing male humpback whales can communicate with distant whales, even in darkness or murky water.

# ECHOLOCATION

**Now we come to a sensory faculty with which we and most other land animals are unfamiliar. Only bats, some shrews and a few cave-dwelling birds could properly appreciate the the developments that have taken place in some cetaceans relating to sound perception of the environment.**

**Cetacean radar** Equivalent to radar or sonar, echolocation is the production of sound, the returning echoes of which give the animal an acoustic "picture" of some parts of its environment. They must be loud enough for the echoes to return to the animal, and short enough so that the echo of one returns before the next one is sent out. The clicks are emitted in a "train." These may be widely spaced while scanning, but as the whale or dolphin approaches a target, the interval between the clicks may shorten until the train sounds rather like a buzzing creak. Higher frequencies may be used at a shorter range, as these probably give superior image resolution.

**Processing signals** It is impossible to know how whales process the information that echolocation gives them. The auditory centers in toothed whale brains are very well developed, indicating that complex processing of sound occurs. As humans rely so heavily on the sense of sight,

**ALWAYS ON THE LOOKOUT**
Even during normal swimming, with no specific target of interest, dolphins, such as these short-beaked common dolphins, use a general low-frequency echolocation signal of fairly pure tone.

we find it hard to imagine "sound pictures." Yet sound may well convey more complex information than light and, by echolocating, whales may experience three-dimensional images of a richness comparable to those produced by human sight.

**Range and limitation** In bottlenose dolphins, echolocation seems to be effective at least as far as 2,500 feet (762 m), and possibly farther in this or other species. The significance of such a sense is clear—in darkness or in murky water, cetaceans can scrutinize objects on the sea floor and locate and track prey and predators. One drawback is that echolocation operates only in a narrow beam directly ahead of the animal. However, a wider target can be covered by swinging the head from side to side. River dolphins do this lying on their sides in order to scan the full depth of shallow water.

### A DOLPHIN ECHOLOCATES

Echolocation clicks are produced in the upper nasal passages and then focused ahead into a narrow directional beam. The front of the skull may act as a parabolic reflector, but focusing seems mainly to occur in the bulbous fat-filled melon, which can probably change shape to alter the beam's focus. The returning echoes are received through a narrow lower jaw, part of which contains fat. It is speculated that the teeth of some species may act as an "acoustic window" for receiving sound.

outgoing
signals

returning
echoes

*The beluga's melon is more prominent than that of many other toothed whales.*

**Discriminating** Studies of captive dolphins show that they can use echolocation with great ability to discriminate among several objects that differ only subtly from each other. These include metal balls made of similar material but of slightly different sizes. Dolphins also demonstrate a capacity to differentiate between hollow and solid balls, and between balls that have different surface textures. Dolphins can even distinguish between balls that are the same size but are made from metals of different densities.

**Advantages** The advantages that dolphins derive from these abilities are tremendous. For example, they can distinguish between the shapes and textures of toxic and non-toxic fish. It also appears that they can employ echolocation to track fast-moving objects with ease.

**Switching on and off** Most toothed whales have very good sight and hearing, so there is no need for them to echolocate all the time. Much of their time is spent simply listening to the ambient sounds of the ocean. This may explain why many cetaceans drown in monofilament gillnets, which their echolocation is perfectly capable of detecting.

**BALEEN WHALES**
Do baleen whales use some form of echolocation? While they lack the specialized anatomical adaptations, such as a melon, that enable toothed whales to detect small, fast-moving prey, they undoubtedly have very good hearing, and may detect their prey passively, or by a relatively crude form of echolocation.

## HEAD STRUCTURE

The skull, both jaws and particularly the large deposits of fat in the melon and the lower jaws—a feature that is unique in the animal kingdom—all play vital roles in a toothed whale's capacity to use echolocation. The chemical composition of the fat deposits is markedly different from that of the normal body fat and from that of the animal's normal dietary fat intake.

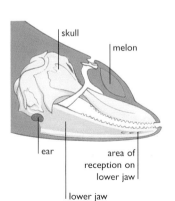

skull

melon

ear

area of reception on lower jaw

lower jaw

Echolocation might be "switched on" only when interesting sounds have been heard, or when prey animals have been sighted by eye.

**Sperm whales** During feeding dives, sperm whales echolocate much of the time, with occasional intriguing silences. Their normal clicks may occur once a second or so, but every so often the rate will increase until there is a "creak" like a squeaking hinge, then silence before the normal clicking resumes. The increased click rate may signal the approach of a squid, and the final buzzing creak could represent the last few feet of increasing short-range echolocation before the squid is seized. From what is known of dolphin echolocation, a sperm whale is likely to be able to tell the direction, size, shape and species of its prey, even at some considerable distance.

73

# HOW WHALES MOVE

As you watch a whale swim, it seems to move effortlessly, but this is misleading. Whales require a great deal of energy to move their large bodies through the water—but they use this energy more efficiently than most other animals. Water provides resistance to movement, and whales overcome this in interesting ways.

**Well-designed bodies** Until recently, scientists were puzzled by the speeds at which some dolphins were able to travel. According to the scientists' calculations, these dolphins possessed only a fraction of the amount of muscle they should have needed to move so fast. Like well-designed ships, whales' bodies produce "laminar flow," which means that the fluid they displace when they move flows smoothly from their front to their rear, producing minimum drag or turbulence. This enables whales to swim relatively fast and for long periods with relatively little exertion. The streamlined

## SWIFT MOVERS
Within their range, Pacific white-sided dolphins can often be seen swimming swiftly and efficiently in groups of up to 100 individuals.

*The flukes begin descending to start the downstroke*

*The downstroke continues*

*The downstroke is completed*

*The upstroke then begins*

*Completing the upstroke*

**FALSE KILLER WHALE**
The false killer whale's long, slender head and slim body are well suited to this animal's style of fast, acrobatic swimming. These whales often breach.

shape of the cetacean's body—in which all the protruding parts, such as hair, external ear pinnae, mammary glands and reproductive organs are reduced or tucked away—and its smooth, rubbery, flexible skin, which has few folds or wrinkles, promote laminar flow, at least as far back as the shoulder, the widest part of the body. Behind the shoulder, turbulence may form, but even this, for technically complex reasons, may ultimately reduce overall drag.

**DOLPHIN PROPULSION**
Cetaceans derive their propulsive power from the vertical flexing of the body and tail flukes; they use the pectoral fins for steering. Until recently, scientists thought that most power was produced during the upstroke, which occurs as the flukes are lifted by the contraction of the large muscles on top of the backbone. However, it now seems possible that the downstroke may be of equal importance, and that it is not, as was believed, merely a passive return to the start of a new upstroke.

# HOW WALES MOVE continued

**The role of skin** Certain properties of cetacean skin could also contribute to reducing drag. When swimming at speed, or during rapid maneuvers (when turbulence develops) temporary ridges form in the

*Dall's porpoise*

skin. These may absorb and reduce the energy of the turbulence, eliminating it before it is fully developed. Such an explanation, however, is highly speculative, and it is possible that these folds could *increase* drag. Also, the outer layer of a whale's

skin contains oily compounds, which may "lubricate" the body as it moves through the water.

**Shedding skin** A whale sheds and renews its outer skin cells rapidly—every couple of hours, compared with every 18 hours in human skin. This could increase the body's streamlining by limiting the growth of barnacles and other parasites that induce drag.

**Secreting mucus** Cetaceans have a large number of glands in their eyelids that produce a copious mucous secretion. This is easily visible as stringy material emerging from the eye and passing back along the body toward the shoulders. This may have a similar function to the fine film of mucus secreted by fish as they swim.

**Porpoising** Dolphins, and some other small cetaceans, use several methods to increase their speed or reduce effort, such as bowriding or porpoising. Porpoising is the name given to the rhythmic

---

**SPRINT CHAMPION**

Dall's porpoises are the fastest-swimming cetaceans. They have been recorded swimming at more than 31 miles (50 km) per hour, although most species commonly cruise at between 5.5 miles (9 km) and 10.5 miles (17 km) per hour. Baleen whales pursued by whalers have attained 18.6 miles (30 km) per hour, possibly in desperation, and there have been some impressive feats of strength and endurance—a fin whale, for example, traveled 2,300 miles (3,700 km) at an average of 10.5 miles (17 km) per hour.

### ENERGY SAVERS

The porpoising short-beaked common dolphins shown here are just one of 33 identified species of oceanic dolphins. Their fishlike shape, smooth skin and flattened tails mean that they can swim at high speed, while still conserving energy. Some dolphins have been recorded swimming at 25 miles (40 km) per hour for several hours.

leaping of dolphins in the air. This is the most efficient way to travel in terms of energy. While they are in the air, dolphins are free of water resistance and so can breathe efficiently while moving at high speed. This helps them to conserve energy. Oceanic dolphins are constantly on the move in search of scattered prey, and they often porpoise while traveling. A high degree of synchronization is often seen among porpoising animals, and it is a spectacular sight when large schools of dolphins are on the move

**Bowriding** Dolphins often use the water displaced by a boat or a large whale to enhance their speed, by bowriding on the pressure wave that it creates. You may see them jostling for position, each seeking to occupy the point at which the wave has optimum thrust.

# BREATHING, DIVING AND BLOWING

You may well be unaware that a whale is close to you until you see or hear its blow. When a whale exhales, its pent-up breath can emerge loudly and explosively. The spectacular sight and sound of the tell-tale spout was once eagerly sought by whalers; today, whale-watching enthusiasts look out for it with equal anticipation. Observers can often identify a whale's species by the size, shape and angle of its blow.

## Breathing and blowholes

Unlike humans, cetaceans control their breathing voluntarily, but they need to surface regularly in order to breathe. The blowhole is often the first part of a whale to appear above the surface. When it blows, a whale expels a cloud of vapor that forms when condensed air from the lungs, combined with oil droplets from inside the breathing passage and also water lying around the blowholes, meets cooler, outside air. After it blows, a whale immediately inhales very rapidly before diving again.

### SURFACING FOR AIR

A bulky humpback whale, with its characteristic knobbly, barnacle-covered skin, brings its head above the surface in order to breathe in air through its pair of blowholes.

**DIVER INTERVAL**

Diving and breathing patterns vary between species, and also depend on the animal's level of activity. Each small "crest" represents a whale surfacing in order to breathe. The vertical scale does not show the great depths—10,000 feet (3,040 m)—to which the sperm whale is able to dive. The horizontal scale shows time elapsed during a dive, but not the distance covered, which may vary.

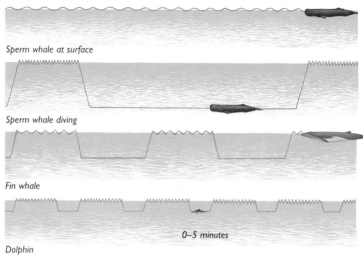

*Sperm whale at surface*

*Sperm whale diving*

*Fin whale*

0–5 minutes

*Dolphin*

**Breathing patterns**

Whales' breathing patterns vary according to species, and are influenced by how active an individual is. While resting at the surface a whale may blow quietly and invisibly, but when swimming fast, it can begin to blow while it is still underwater, and then inhale as soon as its blowhole breaks the surface.

**Lungs** The size of a cetacean's lungs is small in relation to the animal's overall size. Instead of relying on large lung capacity, whales exchange gases very efficiently, replacing about 80 percent of the air in their lungs every time they blow and inhale. In this respect they are about three times as efficient as humans and other land mammals.

## BREATHING, DIVING AND BLOWING continued

**Storing oxygen** Cetaceans also transport and store oxygen very efficiently in their bodies. They have proportionately more blood than other mammals. Blood makes up 10–15 percent of their body weight, compared with about 7 percent in humans. They also have a richer supply of the two proteins that store oxygen: hemoglobin in the blood, and myoglobin in the muscles. Myoglobin has a greater affinity for oxygen than hemoglobin, so oxygen carried in the blood is readily given up to the muscles. Myoglobin is more abundant and more concentrated in whales than in land mammals, giving the cetacean muscles a characteristic dark burgundy color.

**Diving ability** A number of physiological mechanisms enable whales to dive and remain underwater for long periods. As they dive, they are able to slow their heartbeat, and in doing so, save oxygen. At the same time, blood flows away from the non-essential organs and toward vital ones, such as the heart and brain.

**Pressure** Water pressure increases with depth, which poses a known danger to human divers. Whales, however, have developed a remarkable ability to avoid "the bends," which can occur when pressurized air enters the bloodstream. As a diver ascends, the water pressure decreases and the dissolved nitrogen component of the air expands. If it expands

**EMERGING HUMPBACK**
When a humpback whale surfaces, its splashguard and blowholes are the first to appear above the surface. Next, its low, stubby dorsal fin comes into view, and its distinctive sloping back forms a shallow triangle against the surface of the water. As the humpback arches its body, forming a much higher triangle, the hump on its back becomes evident.

### BRIEFLY AT THE SURFACE

The amount of time spent underwater varies greatly among different species, but these Baird's beaked whales, like all cetaceans, require a remarkably brief time at the surface to take in air, partly thanks to the convenient location of their blowholes on the top of the head.

too quickly, dangerous bubbles form in the diver's blood and tissues. But when a whale dives, the increasing water pressure causes its lungs to collapse, and the remaining air is driven into the windpipe, where little of it can find its way into the bloodstream. Also, as a whale dives, blood flows into the small cavities inside the ear, equalizing the pressure in the inner and outer ear. By contrast, human divers must constantly equalize the air pressure in their sinus cavities while descending and ascending.

### DIVE SEQUENCES

The diagram at left shows the characteristic dive sequences of the minke, humpback, southern right and sperm whales. Dive sequences are often a useful tool for identification purposes. The minke is the only one of these species that hardly ever lifts its flukes on a dive. By contrast, the sperm whale's deep vertical dive is preceded by a spectacular vertical lift of its flukes.

Minke

Humpack

Southern right

Sperm

# WHALE BEHAVIOR

The social organization of cetaceans is often a consequence of the ecology of their prey, and the degree of cooperation that they need to employ in order to catch it efficiently. One of the most fascinating things about watching cetaceans is observing the way they interact with each other. Some significant factors that appear to affect the social behavior of cetaceans include habitat; rates and types of predation; the quality and spacing of food patches (and the ease with which they can be located); and the constraints placed on mammals in an aquatic environment. Mothers and calves form the basic unit of society common to all cetacean species, but beyond this differences start to emerge.

# HUNTING AND FEEDING

Feeding is probably the most important factor in determining the nature of cetacean societies. The greatest division is between baleen whales and toothed whales. One group has baleen plates, used to swallow large numbers of small schooling prey; the other has teeth, to grasp single, larger prey.

**Toothed whales** Toothed whales feed mainly on cephalopods (squid, octopus and cuttlefish) and fish. although some species also prey on warm-blooded animals. Others, such as belugas, sometimes forage for bottom-dwelling worms and crustaceans. Most dolphins use their conical, pointed teeth to grasp slippery prey such as fish, which they then swallow whole. Porpoises, on the other hand, may dismember their prey with their slicing teeth.

**FIERCE PREDATOR**
Orcas, or killer whales, are undoubtedly highly intelligent animals. Like dogs or lions, they hunt in groups, and will often come right up on to a beach to catch warm-blooded seals, which are their preferred prey.

Most beaked whales have no functional teeth. In mature male strap-toothed whales, two teeth protrude upward from the lower jaw, folding round the upper jaw and preventing the mouth from opening more than a few inches.

**Suction** Recently it has been discovered that whales without functional teeth actually use suction to capture squid and fish. By rapidly distending the throat grooves and moving the tongue backward like a piston, beaked whales such as Hubb's beaked whale create a powerful suction in their mouths, causing nearby fish, in an observer's words, to "vanish."

**WRAP-AROUND TEETH**
The protruding, upward-growing teeth of a mature male strap-toothed whale greatly inhibit the whale's ability to open its mouth. Even so, these whales continue to feed effectively.

**Toothed but toothless**
Teeth, however, are not essential to toothed whales. Whalers have caught sperm whales which had deformed jaws, but were otherwise in excellent physical condition.

**SPERM WHALE FEEDING**
Sperm whales dive vertically to levels where squid congregate, down to 10,000 feet (3,000 m). Squid can exceed 30 feet (9 m) and whales often swallow them intact. How large, slow-moving sperm whales subdue and swallow such large prey is a mystery. The white pigment around their mouths may act as a lure. A quick suction action may also be used once the squid is within range.

85

**ORCA ATTACK**
This etching shows a group of orcas attacking a solitary bowhead whale. Orcas typically divide the labor in such attacks, each performing a separate task, some herding the victim while others attack.

**Group feeding** A fascinating aspect of toothed whales' behavior is their ability to coordinate group activities. Sometimes, for example, a pod of bottlenose dolphins will encircle a school of fish; or a family of orcas will divide the labor, each performing a separate task as the group harasses and attacks a solitary baleen whale, tearing away pieces of its flesh. It has recently been discovered that false killer whales also attack other whales in this way.

**Herding prey** Herding prey is another way in which toothed whales cooperate in feeding. Many species herd their prey against the surface or against the shore before devouring it. Bottlenose dolphins take this to extremes, by sliding up onto mud banks to catch fleeing fish. Other

## EXCEPTIONS

Given certain examples of sophisticated behavior in whales, it is no surprise that most toothed whales cooperate in their hunting. Some species, however, do not conform to the group feeding pattern and seem to be solitary hunters. Male sperm whales in polar waters are an example of lone feeding activity.

species, such as the dusky dolphin, herd baitfish into tight balls, and take turns to dash in and feed on them.

**Baleen feeding** Filter feeding is linked to many aspects of baleen whale structure and behavior, such as the huge head and mouth, large body, migration pattern and polar feeding. Although they are enormous creatures, baleen whales feed on tiny prey, filtering food from huge volumes of water in a remarkable harvesting operation.

**Baleen plates** Baleen whales filter feed using baleen plates that hang from the roof of the mouth. Each baleen plate is thin, wide and long, shaped like a narrow-based triangle and formed of tough, flexible organic material similar to human hair and nails. Different species have varying numbers, sizes and colors of baleen plates (light, dark or mixed).

### A HUMPBACK FEEDING DIVE

Some baleen whales dive vertically to feed, surfacing near where they started their dive. Others may feed while on the move. Feeding dives are usually of short duration, with dive length related to the depth at which food is found.

A humpback whale surfaces to blow several times prior to a feeding dive

The flukes are raised as the whale begins its steep descent.

Using its hearing or other senses, the whale locates and moves toward a patch of zooplankton.

On reaching the patch, the whale engulfs a mouthful of plankton and water.

After straining and swallowing its prey, the whale returns to the surface to breathe.

**Locating prey** Although baleen whales eat up to 4 percent of their body weight each day, we do not yet know exactly how they locate their prey. Perhaps they listen for the minute rustling and clicking made by a swarm of krill, or they may simply recognize locations and conditions in which such swarms are likely to occur. It is possible that they are able to "taste" their prey in the water, or they may even use a crude form of echolocation, although this still remains to be proven.

**Staying near the surface**
All the baleen whales depend for survival on searching out massive concentrations of the very small organisms on which they feed, and the method of filtration used by each species differs according to their diet. Since dense swarms

of suitable plankton occur mainly in the upper layers of the sea, baleen whales tend to travel mainly near the surface in the top 330 feet (100 m), and to be more shallow in both their cruising and feeding movements than the deep-diving sperm or bottlenose whales. They therefore do not need to spend as much time on each dive.

**FOOD FOR HUMPBACKS**
In Antarctic waters humpbacks feed mainly on krill, but in the Northern Hemisphere they also take a variety of small schooling fish, such as herring, sand lance and capelin. Predominantly gulp feeders, they employ an ingenious variety of feeding techniques, depending on the location and prey. In some places, they even stun the krill or fish with slaps of their pectoral fins or tail flukes.

## NETS OF BUBBLES

One of the most extraordinary feeding techniques is employed by humpbacks. It is known as "bubblenetting." In this process humpbacks produce columns of bubbles from their blowholes. These work just like conventional fishing nets, and trap the prey inside.

**Baleen feeding techniques** "Skimming" and "gulping" are the two main feeding strategies that are employed by baleen whales. Right whales, including the bowhead and the sei whale, are skimmers. These whales feed almost continuously, moving slowly at or near the surface, and forcing a stream of water across their very long baleen plates to skim off food. Gulpers, such as most of the rorquals, tend to feed in dramatic bursts, lunging at shoals of prey with their lower jaw dropped and their mouth wide open, allowing them to engulf a huge volume of water and prey. The gray whale, on the other hand, is unique among whales in that it is predominantly a bottom feeder, scouring the sand and mud and sucking up benthic amphipods. The humpback whale, which is mainly a gulper, also occasionally feeds on the bottom.

# MATING AND REPRODUCTION

All cetacean species have evolved a unique combination of timing, behavioral strategies and physiological adaptations to ensure that they survive. No cetaceans pair for life. Most species are promiscuous, with both males and females having more than one mate.

**Low rates** Compared to many other mammals, cetaceans have low reproductive rates. This is because they grow slowly and do not mature sexually for at least five or six years. The single calf that is born takes a year or more to reach independence. This low rate of reproduction is offset by the fact that whales are generally long-lived. As well, females are capable of bearing many calves during their lifetime.

**RARE TWINS**
Twin calves, such as these young bottlenose dolphins, are a most unusual sight. Multiple births may occur among cetaceans, but they are extremely rare. Even twins, let alone triplets or quadruplets, are rarely reared successfully.

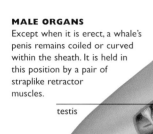

## MALE ORGANS

Except when it is erect, a whale's penis remains coiled or curved within the sheath. It is held in this position by a pair of straplike retractor muscles.

testis

genital slit

penis

anus

fallopian tube

uterus

ovary

cervix

vagina

genital slit

## FEMALE ORGANS

These are similar to those of many other mammals. Toothed whales' ovaries are egg-shaped and smooth. Those of baleen whales are irregular in shape and have protuberances.

### Breeding cycle

From scientific study of the ovaries and testes of dead cetaceans, it appears that reproduction is a cyclical activity. In many species the breeding cycle is intimately linked to the seasons and, in the case of migratory species, to migration. This is particularly so in baleen whales, which have a surge in hormonal activity in both sexes as they approach the breeding areas, possibly stimulated by changes in day length or water temperature. The exception is the tropical Bryde's whale, which breeds throughout the year. Some oceanic dolphins have two breeding peaks—in spring and in fall. Other species, such as coastal bottlenose dolphins, may breed throughout the year, as their environment changes little with the seasons.

## MATING AND REPRODUCTION continued

**Linked cycles** The link between the breeding and migratory cycles means that the breeding season is short and intense. The gestation period in many species is usually around 12 months, so mating occurs on the calving grounds. The female will return a year later to deliver her calf. Huge energy demands on breeding females mean that only very rarely do they breed in consecutive years. More often, there is a breeding cycle

**MULTIPLE PARTNERS**
No cetaceans are monogamous. They are either promiscuous (males and females have multiple partners, as is common among right and gray whales and many dolphins), or polygynous (males mate with multiple females, as seen among sperm whales, orcas and narwhals).

**BREAKING THE TIES**
Female southern right whales appear at the breeding grounds with their calves exactly 12 months after giving birth. Then they simply leave their calves and depart. At this point the calves become juveniles and appear to have little further contact with their mothers.

of two to three years in baleen whales. In many toothed whales, the cycle is even longer.

**Humpback mating rituals** When they seek to mate, male humpbacks advertise their presence with song, and a female chooses her "principal escort." No one knows on what criteria a female bases her choice. Other males attempt to displace him in violent competition

involving head-butting, fluke slapping and jostling. Less rough courtship behaviors, such as slow slapping of pectoral fins, help to synchronize the prospective mate's mood and behavior with that of her suitor.

**FAST GROWER**
On average, a humpback calf is about 14 feet (4.3 m) long at birth—about one-third the length of its mother. However, nourished by its mother's milk, the newborn calf quickly grows.

**Other baleen whales** Gray whales form mating groups consisting of a female and several males. These groups break up when the female has mated with most, if not all, the males. Male southern right whales use a system called "sperm competition." They have by far the largest testes of any animal and produce copious amounts of sperm. Over several weeks, many males will copulate many times with each receptive female and then let their sperm fight it out on the way to the ovum. There is much activity, but no aggression as with humpbacks, and some males even seem to assist each other by restricting the movements of females.

**Toothed whale mating** The breeding behavior of most toothed whales remains a mystery. Male bottlenose dolphins often mate cooperatively, joining forces to herd and subdue females, sometimes treating them roughly, with frequent pushing, biting and vocal threats. Male narwhals use their tusks to duel for access to females. The scars on the bodies of many beaked whales suggest that they too may engage in boisterous or even violent male-to-male competition, although these scars could be inflicted during courtship and mating. Male sperm whales usually travel singly or occasionally in pairs among nursery schools, mating with all the available receptive females before moving on to other schools.

# WHALE INTELLIGENCE

**Cetaceans are usually described as "intelligent mammals." Yet there is a continuing debate about their level of intelligence between those who are convinced they are as intelligent as humans and others who would rank them considerably lower.**

**Large brains** What evidence is there for high cetacean intelligence? Cetaceans have relatively large brains, with considerable development of the cerebral cortex. This is the region associated with higher functions, such as learning and abstract thought. While this could suggest high intelligence, it is counter-argued that large brains are required simply to coordinate their large bodies' motor processes. Even then, the ratio of brain-to-body size in some cetaceans, such

### PERFORMING TRICKS

Bottlenose dolphins in aquariums have been taught to perform many kinds of routines and to respond to signals and verbal instructions. False killer whales are another species that have been taught to perform complex tasks in captivity.

## HUMAN AND CETACEAN BRAINS

The brain on the left is a human brain; the one on the right is the brain of a bottlenose dolphin. What can we make of similarly large and complex brains? In humans, brain complexity and intelligence are apparently linked with sophisticated language and with manipulation of the environment. Cetaceans don't modify their environment in the human sense nor, indeed, as other mammals do, and a human-like language has not been demonstrated. Brain complexity perhaps relates to sound processing, but it is not clear why brains should be similarly complex in toothed and baleen whales, which produce and use different sorts of sounds.

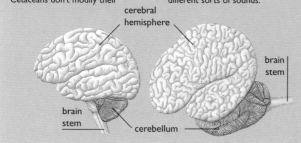

**LANGUAGE LEARNERS?**
So far attempts to teach bottlenose dolphins to understand human language have not progressed very far, though they seem to understand such concepts as "sameness" or "difference."

as large baleen whales, is not high. Sperm whales have the largest brains of all, but bottlenose dolphins have the highest brain-to-body size ratio.

**Skills and awareness** Dolphins are known to use tools, such as wearing a sponge to protect their beaks when foraging in sand. It is tempting to infer near-human intelligence from this. However, many other animals use tools and this is not generally put forward as evidence that they have an intelligence level that comes anywhere near that of humans.

# COMMUNICATION

**Whales have exploited the sound-carrying properties of water by developing superior acoustic communication abilities. Their sounds range from the ultrasonic moans of blue whales to the high-frequency clicks of some dolphins.**

**High and low** Although both ends of the frequency spectrum are beyond the range of human hearing, many whale sounds are clearly audible to us. Baleen whales probably use their larynxes to produce sounds that are generally of lower frequencies than the sounds made by toothed whales. The low-frequency sounds of blue and fin whales may travel hundreds or even thousands of miles. This raises interesting questions about our concept of what constitutes a whale group, which may be defined as a number of animals in contact with each other. All whales use sound to varying degrees in order to communicate.

**Whistling whales**
Most toothed whales produce two basic types of communicative sounds: whistles and clicks. Bottlenose dolphins, and probably many other species, use "signature whistles," unique to individual animals. Constant whistling in gregarious species may be an ongoing "roll call," by which animals signal their presence.

**SOCIAL DOLPHINS**
Fraser's dolphins are a sociable species. They frequently travel in very large groups—up to 1,000 individuals—and can also often be seen feeding and communicating with other species of tropical toothed whales.

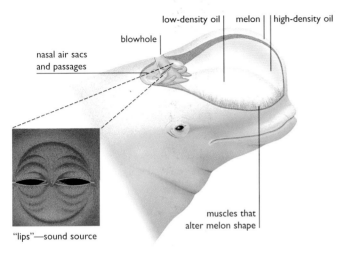

nasal air sacs and passages

blowhole

low-density oil | melon | high-density oil

muscles that alter melon shape

"lips"—sound source

**SOUND PRODUCTION**

Left: We are still learning how sounds are produced by belugas, but the high-frequency sounds in echolocation are probably focused in the melon. As a group, cetaceans produce sounds that range from very high to very low frequencies.

Below: Dolphins, such as common dolphins, produce high-frequency whistles, squeaks and clicks. Splashes and slaps made by the body may also be used in communication.

**Clicks** While clicks are used by all toothed whales for the purposes of echolocation, they may also be used for communication. Along with porpoises, sperm whales are one of the few species known to use clicks exclusively. They seem to communicate using patterns of clicks known as "codas." Some of these codas may be individual signatures, while others appear to be shared by more than one animal. Their meaning remains unknown, except to whales.

97

# COMMUNICATION continued

**Whalesong** The extraordinary songs of humpback whales are uniquely elaborate and complex, although humpbacks can also use simpler sounds to communicate. Humpback songs show regional "dialects," and other species show similar variation. Blue whales have a very simple "song" consisting of as few as four drawn-out notes, the context of which is uncertain. Right whales are more taciturn, uttering the odd moan, belch and grunt. Bowheads are more vocal, and scientists can count how many whales are present by the sounds they make while they are migrating.

### SOUND ON PAPER

Converting sound to marks on paper, this sonogram graphically represents a sequence of humpback whale songs. Researchers invent their own terms to describe sounds.

### COORDINATING

Orcas are a highly social species. It seems that they use their calls to coordinate hunting behavior and to maintain contact with other members of their pod.

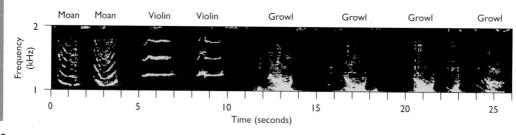

## HUMPBACK SONGS

Humpback whalesong consists of fixed sequences of what have been described as "farmyard" sounds—moans, grunts, chirps and whistles. They may last from 5 to 15 minutes before being repeated many times, often for hours.

Whalesong commonly occurs on breeding grounds and during migration, and very rarely on feeding grounds. Singing is almost invariably the preserve of males, and is thought to be used to court females. It is probably audible to other whales for many miles. Each migratory population has a unique song, sung by all its singers with slight individual variations.

There may be similarities among the songs of different populations living in the same ocean basin, supporting other evidence that animals of different populations mingle in feeding areas. Songs of populations occupying different oceans or hemispheres, however, are commonly quite different from one another.

Whalesongs are constantly evolving as minor modifications are made. How and why these changes occur and are transmitted through a population remain a mystery.

## Non-vocal communication

Whales also use their bodies extensively to convey a wide variety of meaning to each other. There is a spectrum of subtlety in non-vocal communication. At one end is the breach—the most spectacular behavior of all. Many species breach, from dolphins to blue whales. On the other hand, cetaceans frequently communicate with the gentlest of touches, or the subtlest of gestures, such a gentle flick of the tail.

**Acrobatics**  Considerable energy is needed to breach, and one wonders at the meaning of a humpback breaching as many as 100 times consecutively. Perhaps it is an overt warning to another whale or to a boat that has come too close, or it may signal the breacher's presence in rough conditions where vocalizations cannot be heard. Many species use other "aerial" behaviors, such as slapping the tail flukes (lobtailing) or the pectoral fins (pec-slapping) on the water. These are both visual and audible signs that may convey a range of meanings. Both can be leisurely activities and are probably related to courtship.

# SOCIAL BEHAVIOR

The social organization of whales is the link that binds their group structure, behavior and ecology. This complex and fascinating aspect of cetacean life is largely determined by three main priorities: The need to find food, to reproduce their kind and to avoid being preyed upon.

**Group size** Group size among cetaceans is fluid in many species, but in most cases, the larger the gathering of prey, the larger the group will be. Formation of groups also facilitates mating, and there is safety in numbers when predators are about.

**Baleen whales** Baleen whales are usually seen in groups of fewer than 10, and many scientists have concluded that small groups are the norm for these whales. Yet the numbers of most baleen species are still so reduced by whaling

### GROUP TRAVELERS
Schools of several hundred striped dolphins may often be observed traveling in the world's warmer waters, frequently performing striking acrobatics. Smaller groups of these dolphins are also common.

Short-beaked common dolphins (left) can form groups as large as 2,000 or as little as 10. Groups of Atlantic humpback dolphins (below) rarely exceed 25.

that reported sightings may have created a false picture of their societies. There are historical accounts of feeding groups of up to 100 northern right whales, and recently a group of 80 pygmy right whales was sighted. In 1996, 25 blue whales were seen feeding in a localized area off Antarctica.

**Social ties** Humpbacks and southern right whales, the best studied baleen whales, are now revealing unexpectedly subtle and complex social ties. Recent studies

have shown that humpbacks, instead of making short-term associations, form cooperative relationships that endure for many years. Usually these are between females, or between a male and a female. Male right whales in breeding areas form alliances in order to help each other to mate, while mothers associate with other preferred cows and calves.

**Toothed whales** Toothed whale groups are generally larger and more stable than groups of baleen whales. Coastal dolphins, with more patchy prey and more exposure to predators, form large groups that overlap—and interbreed—along coastlines. Oceanic dolphins travel in small, stable pods that amalgamate into large, temporary herds, often hundreds strong, seeking patches of widely dispersed prey and facing many predators, such as sharks. River dolphins, which face few predators and have evenly dispersed prey, occur in small groups, or singly.

*Atlantic humpback dolphin*

## SOCIAL BEHAVIOR continued

### Matrilineal societies

Most toothed whale societies are female-based, or matrilineal. With few exceptions—orcas and pilot whales are two such exceptions—males leave their mother's group when they reach sexual maturity, and join other groups. Mating occurs when such groups meet at sea, so an individual's chances of mating are increased if it is part of such a group. Male sperm whales leave their mother's group when they reach about 10 years of age. They then join bachelor groups and remain there until they are about 27—at which point they are large enough to compete sexually. Female sperm whales stay with their mother's group for the whole of their lives; their calves are cared for by the entire "nursery school."

**LARGE HERDS**
Melon-headed whales, like many other members of the family Delphinidae, generally travel in large, tightly packed herds. In the case of this species these groups usually number between 100 and 500, but occasionally herds of 1,500 to 2,000 are encountered.

**Exceptions** Orcas and pilot whales are among the rare exceptions to this female-centered rule. In these species, all members remain with one group for life, and mating occurs between two such groups. This leads to a very high degree of social cohesiveness and cooperation, which is well demonstrated, for example, in the coordinated and cooperative manner in which orcas often hunt their prey.

**Altruistic or selfish?** Toothed whales may risk their own lives to help, or simply to accompany, a companion in distress. The theory is that such altruistic, or selfless, behavior occurs between closely

**BLUE WHALE**

Blue whales (above) are usually seen feeding alone or in pairs. However, it is possible that these whales are more sociable than these observations suggest. The numbers of blue whales, particularly in the Southern Hemisphere, may have been reduced to such an extent that contact and socializing between them have become difficult to achieve.

related individuals, because by helping one another they are improving the chances of their shared genes surviving. Altruistic behavior appears to be the basis of many mass strandings, where healthy individuals will strand with an ailing companion. Sperm whales were famous among old-time whalers for their habit of defending or accompanying a harpooned pod member. However, toothed whales are by no means always altruistic; in one observed incident, a pod of oceanic dolphins quickly abandoned one group member that had become entangled in a net. Once released, it fled in the direction of its group.

**Status and hierarchies**

Dominance hierarchies, or "pecking orders," in which subordinate animals are forcefully reminded of their place, are clearly seen in captive cetaceans. In the wild, superior status may be expressed in the right of access to important resources such as food, or by segregation of animals in space. In some oceanic dolphins, schools form up to five layers, which re-form after each surfacing—presumably the highest-status animals are closest to the surface, where they expend less energy in breathing. Schools of toothed whales are often segregated according to age or sex.

**Physical aggression** Social status conflicts often become physical. Tooth rake marks are very common in many toothed species, and indicate the frequency of aggressive interactions in everyday life. In some beaked whales, males have a single pair of teeth used for display or fighting, and many animals are covered with linear scars.

# AVOIDING PREDATORS

The natural predators of cetaceans are orcas and sharks. False killer whales and pygmy killer whales have also been observed attacking other cetaceans. No cetacean species (except, perhaps, orcas themselves) is safe from attack from other marine, and even terrestrial, animals.

**Safety in numbers** Forming a group is the most basic defensive cetacean strategy. The detection of predators is enhanced by the combined senses of sight, hearing and echolocation of all the group's members. The larger the group, the lesser are an individual's chances of being preyed upon. Group members often help each other to drive off attackers. Groups of oceanic dolphins, such as spinner and spotted dolphins, sometimes number thousands.

## PROTECTIVE CIRCLE

Sperm whales take up a formation such as this as a defense strategy. As a pod of orcas approaches, adult whales form a circle, with their heads toward the center and their flukes (their defensive weapons) facing outward. Young or wounded animals are placed within the circle. The thrashing tails offer a powerful deterrent to the orcas.

**Small groups** Many species, however, are unable to form large groups for defense. This is largely because their food occurs in small patches, and in large groups, group members might become rivals for food, and therefore attack each other. So the group size of most species depends primarily on the ecology of their prey.

**Fight or flight?** Different strategies may be used when whales are under attack from predators. They may flee or, if they are slow-moving or have young with them, they may stand and fight—or at least attempt to scare their attackers away. Humpbacks have been seen to react to orca attacks with violent fluke thrashing, turning and rolling. Unless it responds very vigorously, there may be little that a solitary baleen whale can do to defend itself against a coordinated attack.

**BELUGA**
Polar bears commonly prey on stranded or young belugas. They often bite or scratch at the beluga's blowhole, so that it cannot breathe.

**Putting up a screen** An extraordinary defensive behavior seen in sperm whales involves throwing up a defensive screen. When threatened, sperm and pygmy sperm whales may emit blinding clouds of feces. Other defensive behaviors include making mock charges, puffing themselves up and making threatening gestures.

# MIGRATION

The distances that many whales cover in the course of a migratory cycle are so great that each year they spend as much time in transit as they do in the feeding and breeding grounds that they travel between. Some whales, on the other hand, travel only short distances in localized areas.

**Seasonal movements** Whales migrate seasonally. During the polar summer, they feed on a rich variety of abundant marine life. In the polar winter, food is scarcer, and many whales move away to breed and rear their young in warmer waters. This movement between feeding and breeding areas is called the migratory cycle.

**Baleen whales** Of all whale migrations, those of baleen whales are the most predictable and the ones that have been most closely observed. But the reasons for these

**MINKE AND SPERM WHALES**
Above: Minke whales that are not involved in breeding often do not migrate, but spend the winter in the Antarctic sea ice.
Left: Regular long-distance migrations are virtually unknown in toothed whales, except for older male sperm whales, which migrate huge distances between feeding and breeding grounds.

## WHALE NAVIGATION

How whales navigate during migrations
is unknown. There are many possible
mechanisms, some of which we know
are used by other migratory animals.
Perhaps over millions of years some of
these strategies have become blended
to give whales a kind of general
navigational awareness. Unraveling the
details is a task for the future.

*Migrating whales may
spyhop to check their
position visually against such
familiar neutral features as
headlands and islands.*

long and arduous journeys are not
clear. It is often assumed that
newborn calves cannot survive in
the cold winter waters and that
reduced food supplies in winter
feeding grounds cannot sustain
the whale populations. But in
Antarctic waters there is ample
food in winter to sustain millions
of seals and penguins, as well as
numerous minke whales.

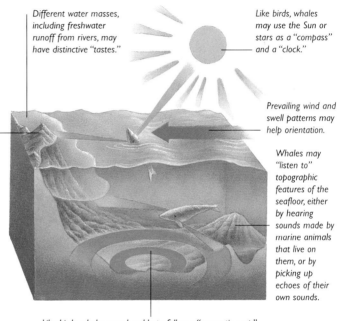

*Different water masses,
including freshwater
runoff from rivers, may
have distinctive "tastes."*

*Like birds, whales
may use the Sun or
stars as a "compass"
and a "clock."*

*Prevailing wind and
swell patterns may
help orientation.*

*Whales may
"listen to"
topographic
features of the
seafloor, either
by hearing
sounds made by
marine animals
that live on
them, or by
picking up
echoes of their
own sounds.*

*Like birds, whales may be able to follow a "magnetic map"
by detecting anomalies in the Earth's magnetic field*

### HUMPBACK MIGRATIONS
Humpback whales commute between extensive summer feeding grounds in polar regions and somewhat more restricted winter breeding grounds in the tropics.

**Darker days** Shortening days may be the trigger for the whales' departure, but other factors may also be significant. Different groups of Southern Hemisphere humpbacks, for example, leave Antarctic waters at different times during fall. The first to leave are females with suckling calves which are on the verge of becoming independent; the last are pregnant females that need to gain extra weight to prepare them for the long journey. After up to three months in the tropics, newly pregnant females leave first,

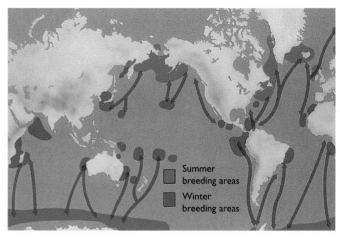

Summer breeding areas

Winter breeding areas

followed by immatures, adult males and, last, cows with calves that are large enough to endure their first migration. Tropical breeding grounds and migration routes are food-poor compared to polar waters, so there is little chance to feed on the move. Migrating whales must subsist for up to eight months on the energy that is stored in their muscle, blubber and body fat.

### Great rorqual migrations

Humpbacks in both hemispheres migrate huge distances. In the North Atlantic, humpbacks from feeding grounds as far apart as Maine in the United States, Greenland and Iceland congregate to breed on shallow banks in the West Indies. Whales from a single Antarctic feeding ground may travel in successive years to South Pacific breeding areas such as New Caledonia and Australia's Great Barrier Reef. Some humpbacks move between Japan, Hawaii and British Columbia. One group, which every year travels from the Antarctic Peninsula across the Equator to Colombia, and back, has the longest regular migration of any mammal. Other rorquals have a similar migratory cycle, though we know little of the routes they take or the location of their breeding grounds. Northern right whales may move from

feeding grounds near Iceland to the east coast of the United States. Southern right whales migrate from the southern continents as far south as the Antarctic ice edge. The formation of sea ice in Arctic waters is the signal for bowheads to move to warmer parts.

### GRAY WHALE MIGRATIONS

Gray whales migrate in shallow coastal waters from their summer feeding grounds in polar seas to calving areas in warm temperate seas. A few grays do not complete their migration if they find sufficent food during the journey.

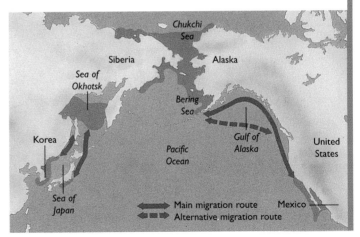

109

**Toothed whales** Many toothed whales are nomadic, rather than truly migratory; their movements are dictated more by changing distributions of prey than by patterns of feeding and breeding. Two migrating species that forsake the polar regions in winter are bottlenose whales and long-finned pilot whales. As the cold sets in, the former set out for the tropics and the latter make for cool temperate regions. Whether a mature sperm whale makes a seasonal move depends on its sex: Females, along with immature males and juveniles, do not move from warmer waters; adult males spend the summer months in polar areas, feeding on squid. We know far less about the migrations of toothed whales than we do about those of baleen whales.

**BELUGAS**

The map below shows the distribution and movements of belugas in Arctic seas. The arrows indicate the directions of the belugas' migrations during spring to main summer feeding areas.

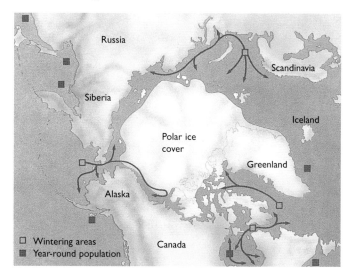

□ Wintering areas
■ Year-round population

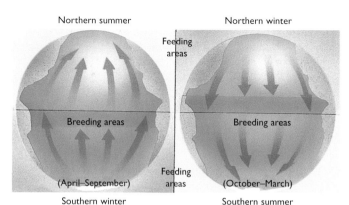

Northern summer

Northern winter

Feeding areas

Breeding areas

Breeding areas

(April–September)

Feeding areas

(October–March)

Southern winter

Southern summer

**BALEEN MIGRATORY PATTERNS**
Left: This diagram shows the general form of the migration of baleen whales. Below: Fin whales are among the fastest and most powerful of migratory travelers. They move between warm tropical waters, such as lagoons in Baja California, Mexico and Alaska. Their migratory routes do not take them close to mainland coasts, and in fact mature individuals, particularly in southern populations, seem to avoid coastal waters altogether. Apparently calves are born in regions of relatively deep water.

**Fast or slow?** Although they travel more or less constantly, both day and night, migrating whales seldom swim non-stop. They may pause to rest, to socialize or even to feed, although this happens rarely. Social interaction is as important to whales when they are traveling as when they are in their feeding and breeding grounds.

During migration, whales are often seen idling or engaging in vigorous pre-mating behavior. Sometimes they will even swim against the flow of migration. There is, therefore, considerable variation in overall migration speeds—from one day to the next, and also between individual groups and different species.

# THE MYSTERY OF STRANDINGS

Most cetaceans die somewhere at sea. The majority probably sink or their carcass is eaten by sharks, but a small proportion, usually solitary animals, are washed ashore by the wind and currents. Causes of death may include disease or shark attack—or simply old age.

**Mass strandings** Single live stranded animals are often old, sick or suffering from injuries and may be too weak to continue swimming. Being air-breathers, perhaps they find a last few hours alive on a beach preferable to drowning. Although most live strandings are of small groups of animals, sometimes a herd of hundreds of toothed whales or dolphins may appear close inshore and then seemingly deliberately beach themselves.

**STRANDED IN FLORIDA**
This whale was washed ashore on a beach in Florida, in the southeastern United States. Single or small group strandings are much more common than mass strandings.

**Species that strand** A wide variety of species is known to strand. However, studies show that species that strand most often, and in greatest numbers, are those that form cohesive social groups and are commonly found in deep water away from coastlines. These include pilot whales, false killer whales and sperm whales. Species of whales that spend much time along coastlines, such as southern right whales and humpbacks, rarely strand.

**Why do they strand?** The once-cherished view that whales are "committing suicide" when they strand is no longer accepted, and other explanations have been proposed. Deepwater species may strand when they find themselves in unfamiliar shallow coastal waters which they have entered in pursuit of prey. Some small cetaceans strand to avoid predators such as orcas. Strandings may also result from disruption to normal navigation. Parasites occurring in the brain or the ears may interfere with the whale's sensory abilities.

**Topographical factors** Physical topography seems a significant factor in strandings, since they are often more concentrated near certain coastal features. In New Zealand, mass strandings are more common where a long, gently sloping beach lies near a protruding headland. The headland may divert whales toward the beach, where the shelving bottom returns no echolocation signals, creating the illusion of open water ahead. Sand bars may compound the confusion, channeling animals into the surf zone where they are driven ashore. Onshore winds and currents may also play a part in strandings of whales.

*A nineteenth-century etching of a solitary stranded right whale.*

113

**Social bonds** Mass strandings demonstrate the strength of close social bonds in toothed whale groups. In some strandings a single animal may be distressed by injury or disease and strand itself. Initially its companions may mill about just offshore, but then often join it in shallow water, and refuse to leave it at their own peril. As the tide falls, these animals become properly stranded. When individual animals are returned to the water, they will often re-strand immediately, possibly because their social bonds are stronger than their aversion to being out of the water. Occasionally, when an entire group is rescued, they may soon re-strand at the same beach, or at another one nearby. Why they do so is a mystery. The worst stranding on record may well be attributable to social bonding. In 1985, a herd of more than 400 long-finned pilot whales stranded in Catherine Bay in New Zealand. While such strandings may be interpreted as either noble or foolish, it is important to realize that the social structures that give rise to them are also the key to survival for these species.

**RARE EVENTS**

Although they are often widely publicized, live stranding are really very rare. For example, in the first 70 years of the United Kingdom's strandings recording system, only 137 records could be identified as live strandings. These included 28 group strandings (with three or more animals involved) and 96 single and pair strandings. The other 13 incidents were near-strandings, with all the preliminary features of live strandings; these ended in the escape of all or most animals.

**LIKELY TO STRAND**
Short-finned pilot whales, deepwater animals that form strong social bonds, are, along with long-finned pilot whales, false killer whales and sperm whales, among those species that are most likely to strand in large numbers.

## HELP FOR THE HELPLESS GIANTS

If you are the first at the scene of a stranding, what can you do? Someone should notify the police or wildlife authorities as soon as possible. Often, the first instinct is to try immediately to return the animal to the sea. Such attempts may injure the whale or it may well end up re-stranding. The following are some guidelines and some first-aid measures you can take to try to stabilize the whale's condition while you are waiting for expert help to arrive.

**Never pull** on the head, dorsal fin, flippers or flukes, but try to roll the animal upright, so that its blowhole is clear of the water or sand.

**Try to orient its body** up the beach, away from the breaking waves. Avoid getting too close to the flukes and the teeth, because a distressed animal may thrash about and injure or bite you.

**Rinse the eyes and blowhole** clear of sand. However, take great care to avoid pouring water or washing sand into the blowhole when it is open.

**Keep the skin from drying out.** You can do this by pouring water over it or, preferably, by covering the animal with a cloth and keeping the cloth damp. Bring buckets and sheets or blankets, if available.

**Remain calm,** and talk to and stroke the whale quietly and reassuringly. Unless spectators are prepared to help, ask them to keep at a distance, and to remain quiet.

**As long as** they are made quite comfortable, and are not bothered by excessive noise or crowds, whales and dolphins can rest comfortably for some time, until other measures can be put in place. They appear to appreciate the efforts made to help them.

**Geomagnetic navigation** A phenomenon that may yet explain many strandings is a geomagnetic navigational sense which, it is thought, cetaceans may possess. Some other animals, such as migratory birds and marine turtles, possess this sense, and magnetite, a mineral involved in geomagnetic navigation in other animals, has been found in the brains of some cetaceans. Such a capability could help to explain the whale's marvelous ability to navigate over great tracts of seemingly featureless ocean. In Britain and the east coast of the United States, strandings have been related to anomalies in the Earth's magnetic field, and there is some other evidence that cetaceans use contours in the field for the purposes of navigation. However, a New Zealand study failed to find any relationship between strandings and magnetic anomalies.

# PART TWO

# KINDS OF
# WHALES

# CLASSIFYING
## AND
# NAMING WHALES

The order Cetacea is divided into three suborders: the archaeocetes (all of which are extinct); the mysticetes (known as baleen whales); and the odontocetes (known as toothed whales). Each of these suborders is further divided into families, genera and, ultimately, species. There are 11 mysticetes. All them are referred to as whales, and every species has "whale" in its common name: blue whale, gray whale, northern right whale, minke whale, Bryde's whale, and so on. The odontocetes, on the other hand, are referred to variously as whales, dolphins or porpoises, depending on a number of different factors. These toothed whales comprise at least 70 widely differing species.

# COMMON AND SCIENTIFIC NAMES

Mention *Balaenoptera musculus* to most people and you will probably be greeted with blank, uncomprehending stares. But the eyes of a group of whale biologists will light up immediately. The reason is simple: *Balaenoptera musculus* is the scientific name for the blue whale.

### Avoiding confusion

Admittedly, "blue whale" is the more appealing of the two names. It is easier to remember and is aptly descriptive, so it is not surprising that most people prefer this "common" name to the scientific one. But common names can cause problems: Many species have common names in different languages, or even alternative names in the same language. For example, the blue whale's close relative, the fin whale, is also known in English as the finback or the finner. To avoid any confusion, it is best to call it *Balaenoptera physalus*, its scientific name.

### BEAKED WHALE

Baird's beaked whale is named after whale researcher Spencer Baird, who became secretary of the Smithsonian Institution in the 1880s.

**MELON HEAD**
The melon-headed whale has a slim, pointed head with a distinctive "melon" shape—hence its common name.

**Name structure** The scientific name of an animal or plant is Latinized and printed in italics (or underlined in handwriting). It normally consists of two different words: The first begins with a capital letter and identifies the genus, while the second begins with a lower-case letter and refers to the species. Occasionally there may be a third word in a scientific name to identify a subspecies (if there is one). As biologists learn more about genetic relationships, new species or subspecies are still being recognized.

**SPEEDY SPRAYER**
The fast-moving Dall's porpoise is named after American zoologist William H. Dall, who first noted its existence in the 1870s. It is also often referred to as the spray porpoise, because of the distinctive spray—sometimes called a "rooster tail" spray—that it pushes up as it rises to the surface to breathe. *Phocoenoides dalli* is its scientific name.

### Classifying the Minke Whale and Humpback Whale

Minke and humpback whales are classified in the following way:

|           | Minke                         | Humpback                      |
| --------- | ----------------------------- | ----------------------------- |
| Kingdom   | Animalia (animals)            | Animalia (animals)            |
| Phylum    | Chordata (chordates)          | Chordata (chordates)          |
| Subphylum | Vertebrata (vertebrates)      | Vertebrata (vertebrates)      |
| Class     | Mammalia (mammals)            | Mammalia (mammals)            |
| Order     | Cetacea (cetaceans)           | Cetacea (cetaceans)           |
| Suborder  | Mysticeti (baleen whales)     | Mysticeti (baleen whales)     |
| Family    | Balaenopteridae (rorquals)    | Balaenopteridae (rorquals)    |
| Genus     | *Balaenoptera*                | *Megaptera*                   |
| Species   | *acutorostrata*               | *novaeangliae*                |

121

# WHALE CLASSIFICATION

Scientific names are important as a means of exact identification and designation of different species of animals or plants. Unique scientific names are also important because they allow scientists to place living things within a structure of relationships in the animal or plant kingdom.

**Taxonomy** Biologists classify all living things by arranging them in groups, according to their similarities and differences. This very specialized science is known as taxonomy.

**Complex family trees** The science of taxonomy is rather like working out an enormously complex family tree. The basic unit is the species, which is defined as a population of animals whose members do not freely interbreed with members of other populations. A genus is simply a group of closely related species. In the same way, a group of closely related genera (plural of genus) forms a family; then closely related families are grouped into orders, closely related orders into classes, and so on.

**Changing names** This method of classification works very well— for most of the time. In practice, though, scientific names and groupings have to be changed as new information comes to light, or when biologists disagree over the details of a particular grouping. It is also necessary, in some cases, to add extra groupings (subspecies, subfamilies and suborders) to deal with more complex relationships within the system.

*Northern right whale*

*Bryde's whale*

**Classifying cetaceans** The real problem faced by taxonomists is in establishing which animals are most closely related. All of the whales, dolphins and porpoises are related to some extent, but clever detective work is needed to determine the different levels of these particular relationships.

## Going by appearances

Taxonomy is an evolving science, and methods of classification have been revised and improved over the years. Early taxonomists classified cetaceans almost entirely on their external appearance, but this was never a satisfactory system. It was almost tantamount to assuming, for example, that all men with bald heads and gray beards must be related, and sometimes resulted in unrelated species being linked and closely related species being kept apart.

## CLASSIFYING BALEEN WHALES

Living cetaceans are all members of the order Cetacea. This order is divided into two suborders, each of which contains several smaller groups, or families. In all, there are 13 families of cetaceans which contain more than 80 different species of whales. The diagram below shows the way researchers have classified the 11 species of baleen whales—members of the suborder Mysticeti—into four family groups. Two of these families contain only a single species. Family names are always recognizable by the Latin plural ending "ae."

**Suborder Mysticeti**

Baleen whales

**Balaenidae**
Right whales and bowhead whale

**Neobalaenidae**
Pygmy right whale

**Eschrichtiidae**
Gray whale

**Balaenopteridae**
Rorquals

**Common dolphins** Common dolphins are an example of debate among scientists leading to a change of classification. For many years, long-beaked and short-beaked common dolphins were considered to be a single species, known generally as common dolphins with the scientific name *Delphinus delphis*. However, differences between various populations led scientists at different times to propose more than 20 separate species for these dolphins. Eventually, in 1994, agreement was reached to create a new species based on anatomy as well as genetics. The new species, the long-beaked common dolphin, was given the scientific name *Delphinus capensis*. The debate is probably not yet over, as even within each species, there are significant variations.

**Gathering information** These days, classification of cetaceans is highly sophisticated. Taxonomists gather information from a wide range of disciplines. These include physiology, behavioral biology, ecology, paleontology and even biochemistry.

**Recent research** Recent work in the field of biochemical research, especially on analyzing DNA (deoxyribonucleic acid), has had a particularly dramatic impact on the classification of the animal

kingdom. In essence, it enables scientists to measure the level of relationships among species in an extraordinarily precise way.

**Using DNA** DNA is the basic genetic material found in all animals. It is a kind of instruction manual for the design and assembly of the body's proteins. Every cell in an animal's body contains an exact replica of this manual, and almost all the "pages" go to making it what it is—a

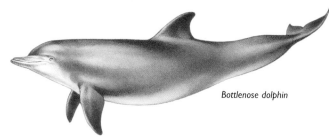

*Bottlenose dolphin*

human, a dog, a humpback whale, a long-snouted spinner dolphin, and so on. The small number of "pages" that are left help to distinguish one individual from another—just as one person's fingerprints are different from everyone else's, so no two animals have exactly the same DNA. Making sense of all the similarities and differences in DNA is an extremely complex process, but it has already resolved a number of long-standing uncertainties in the classification of whales, dolphins and porpoises, as well as many other wildlife species.

**TOOTHED WHALES**

This diagram shows how researchers have classified toothed whales—which belong to the suborder Odontoceti—into 9 families containing more than 70 species. One of these families consists of only a single species.

**Suborder Odontoceti**

Toothed whales

**Physeteridae**
Sperm whale

**Kogiidae**
Pygmy and dwarf sperm whales

**Monodontidae**
White whales

**Ziphiidae**
Beaked whales

**Delphinidae**
Dolphins and other small toothed whales

**Phocoenidae**
Porpoises

**Platanistidae**
Ganges and Indus river dolphins

**Iniidae**
Amazon river dolphins

**Pontoporiidae**
Baiji and franciscana

# BALEEN WHALES

Characterized by the horny plates, known as baleen, that hang from their upper jaw, and through which they filter their food, the four families of baleen whales comprise eleven species. Most are huge, and included amongst them is the blue whale, the largest animal that has ever lived on the Earth. Yet these giants of the oceans feed on some of the tiniest marine creatures. Most baleen whales are long-distance travelers, making seasonal migrations from feeding grounds near the North and South Poles to breeding areas in tropical regions. Some, such as the spectacular humpback whale, every year cover a distance almost equal to half the circumference of the Earth.

# NORTHERN RIGHT WHALE

Right whales were so called because the early whalers considered them the "right" whales to hunt—full of oil and easy to catch. Once victimized by whalers, the northern right whale is today often a victim of its feeding habits. In some prime right whale areas, shipping traffic needs to slow down to avoid these slow-moving whales as they sift copepods from the water.

**Appearance** A series of white skin thickenings, or callosities, or areas of roughened skin, on the head and upper and lower jaw and above the eye are distinctive features that make it difficult to confuse this large, stocky whale with any other. The callosity on the tip of the upper jaw is often called a bonnet. The callosities are all the more prominent because whale lice and occasional barnacles attach themselves to them. This slow-swimming species is mainly black, but may have large white splotches on the belly and chin. Young whales have pale skin, which darkens as they grow to adulthood. Right whales have massive heads, up to one-quarter of the total body length. They lack a dorsal fin, and their pectoral fins are paddle-shaped. The flukes are very long, narrow and pointed.

**Reproduction** Gestation period is unknown, possibly 12 months. Males are sexually mature at 46–50 feet (14–15 m), females at 43–50 feet (13–15 m). Contact between the sexes is restricted to mating. Calving is probably at three-year intervals.

**Comment** The northern right whale is the most endangered whale in the ocean. Its numbers have been reduced to about 300 in the North Atlantic, and possibly to a mere handful in the North Pacific. These whales often breach or roll around in the water.

## KEY FACTS

♀ 59 ft (18 m)

♂ 56-59 ft (17-18 m)

**Other names** Black right whale, Biscayan right whale
**Size at birth** 15–20 ft (4.5–6 m)
**Weight** 40–80 tons/tonnes
**Diet** A specialized feeder; prefers small planktonic animals like copepods
**Group size** 1–3; occasionally larger groups (10–12) form on breeding or feeding grounds
**Habitat** Temperate and subpolar waters; sometimes coastal areas
**Distribution** North Pacific, west coast of USA, Japan and eastern and western sides of the North Atlantic

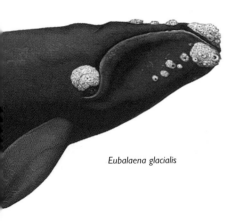

*Eubalaena glacialis*

# Bowhead Whale

Within its home range, the bowhead's sheer size and bulk make it distinctive—the arctic toothed whales, the narwhal and the beluga, are both much smaller. The bowhead spends its life following the advance and retreat of Arctic ice. For the long winter, it lives in total darkness. In the short summer, the 24-hour sunshine brings a brief explosion of life and a world bathed in light.

**Appearance** This large, rotund whale—the stockiest of the baleen whales—has a massive head and a white chin patch. Its color is generally blue-black (in young whales) to blue-gray (in older whales). Like the right whales, it lacks a dorsal fin. The mouthline has a bowed appearance, emphasized by a strongly arched narrow upper jaw. The baleen of bowheads is the longest of any whale; the middle plates may measure 14 feet (4.3 m) and are dark and blackish with fine, paler fringes. Recognition at sea is often by the characteristic bushy V-shaped blow, small paddle-shaped pectoral fins, and pointed flukes. There is what appears to be a light gray to white band around the tail stock. Bowheads can break through sea ice in order to breathe.

**Reproduction** Gestation period is 12–16 months. Males are sexually mature at 37½ feet (11.5 m) and females at 43–46 feet (13–14 m). Calving occurs in mid-winter, when a single young is born. Occasionally, twins are born.

**Comment** Bowhead whales were the second main species—after the right whale—to be targeted by the whaling industry. Driven to commercial extinction, today only a few are taken each year by Inuit and other native people.

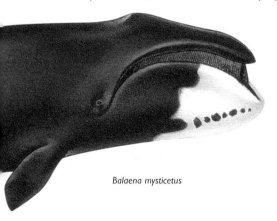

*Balaena mysticetus*

# PYGMY RIGHT WHALE

The pygmy right whale is the sole member of the family Neobalaenidae. It is the smallest of all the baleen whales and is only very distantly related to the right whales. It is called a "right" whale because of the shape of its mouth, which seems to be an example of convergent evolution. In body shape it more closely resembles the minke whale or Bryde's whale.

**Appearance** This small, streamlined animal is rarely sighted at sea. It shares some features with right and bowhead whales, such as a strongly bowed lower jaw, but there are also differences. It possesses a prominent, sickle-shaped dorsal fin, and the pectoral fins are more like those of the rorquals, being narrow and rounded. The flukes are broad. There is no ridge on the rostrum or the back. The body color varies between individuals.

It is generally dark gray on the back, darkening to a deeper gray or black as the animal ages, and a lighter gray or white on the belly. The baleen plates are narrow and number 210–230 on each side. The baleen are yellowish white, with a brown margin, ending in a fringe of fine, soft bristles. The species name of this whale, *marginata,* refers to the marginal band on the baleen.

**Reproduction** Very little information has come to light about the reproductive history, or indeed the lifestyle or the diet, of this rare whale. Females probably calve during the fall–winter period, and it is possible that there is an extended breeding season.

**Comment** Until recently pygmy right sounds were unknown, but hydrophones adjacent to a solitary animal in Victoria, Australia, picked up on several occasions double thumps, like drum beats.

## KEY FACTS

♀ 21 ft (6.5 m)

♂ 20 ft (6 m)

**Other names** None
**Size at birth** Approx. 6½ ft (2 m)
**Weight** Very few have been weighed; ♀ estimated at 3.5 tons/tonnes ♂ estimated at 3.1 tons/tonnes
**Diet** The fine baleen bristles suggest very small prey, such as copepods
**Group size** Mainly single or pairs
**Habitat** Between latitudes of 30°S and 52°S.
**Distribution** Strandings provide the only clues to possible migrations of these whales. Most strandings have occurred on the southern coasts of Australia and South Africa

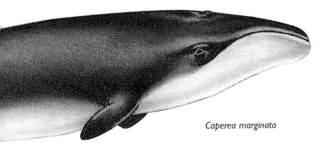

*Caperea marginata*

# GRAY WHALE

The only member of the family Eschrichtiidae, the gray whale was described a "devilish" by whalers, mainly because of the ferocity of the mothers when separated from their calves. Whale watchers are still advised to avoid coming between mothers and calves. Young gray whales, however, are often "friendly," coming to the side of boats and even lifting them out of the water.

**Appearance** The gray whale has a relatively small, narrow, triangular head, a slightly bowed mouth, and small visible hairs in pits on the rostrum. It has a series of bumps along the rear third of the dorsal ridge instead of a true dorsal fin. The flippers are pointed and paddle-like, with a notched tail fluke measuring 10 feet (3 m) from tip to tip. Overall body color is mottled gray with numerous encrusted patches of yellowish white or orange barnacles and whale lice. The extent of these parasites can indicate the general health of an individual. In each side of the upper jaw are 140–180 thick, yellowish white baleen plates that are up to 16 inches (40 cm) long. The blow is "heart-shaped," vertical to about 10–15 feet (3–4.5 m), and loud.

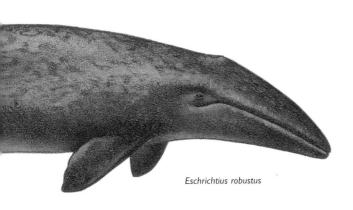

*Eschrichtius robustus*

## KEY FACTS

♀ 46 ft (14.1 m)

♂ 43 ft (13 m)

**Other names**  Mussel digger, hard head, devil fish, gray back
**Size at birth**  15 ft (4.6 m)
**Weight**  14–35 tons/tonnes
**Diet**  A seafloor feeder, eating shrimplike amphipods, polychaete worms and mollusks
**Group size**  Generally 1–3; traveling groups can contain up to 16; hundreds can gather in good feeding conditions
**Habitat**  Coastal waters, usually less than 33 ft (10 m) deep, and above the continental shelf
**Distribution**  Western and eastern sides of the North Pacific

**Reproduction**  Gestation period is about 13.5 months, with approximately two years between pregnancies. Males are sexually mature at 36½ feet (11.1 m) and females at 38½ feet (11.7 m). Young are born during a brief period of five to six weeks beginning in late December.

**Comment**  A North Atlantic population of gray whales was exterminated by whalers in the early eighteenth century, and by the 1930s the species was almost extinct. Now, however, there are more than 20,000 individuals.

# Blue Whale

Almost every aspect of the blue whale's appearance and natural history provides another footnote for the record books. This is the largest living animal, but the largest known blue is subject to debate. The "best" record appears to be at least 110 feet (33.6 m) long and weighing 209 tons (190 tonnes). It was a female—the largest baleen whales are females.

**Appearance** This huge, streamlined, slender whale has a broad, flat, U-shaped head with a single prominent median ridge. A very small dorsal fin of variable shape is located three-quarters to four-fifths of the way along the body. The pectoral fins are pointed and slender, with pale undersides, and the flukes are large and notched. Paired nostrils are located on top of the head with prominent fleshy mounds. True to their name, blue whales are an overall bluish gray, although they can appear mottled and blotched. In polar waters, a browny yellow diatomaceous bloom sometimes covers the skin.

**Reproduction** Gestation period is about 11 months. Males are sexually mature at about 74 feet (22.6 m), females at 79 feet (24 m). It is not a gregarious

whale; mating is probably a temporary arrangement. A single young is born in warm temperate and subtropical waters.

**Comment** At sea, blue whales usually feed alone or in pairs, often widely spaced, probably because they need to work large areas. During the twentieth century, blue whales were pursued relentlessly; by the 1950s, they were endangered. Today, only between 6,000 and 14,000 blue whales are estimated to remain in the world's oceans.

♀ 102 ft (31 m)

♂ 95-98½ ft (29-30 m)

**Other names** Sulfurbottom
**Size at birth** 23 ft (7 m)
**Weight** 100–120 tons/tonnes
**Diet** Swarming euphausiids, in common with many other rorqual whales
**Group size** A solitary animal; paired animals are often a mother and calf
**Habitat** Largely pelagic; rarely seen near the coast; known to follow retreating ice edge in summer
**Distribution** All oceans; frequents low-latitude warm waters (winter), high-latitude waters (summer)

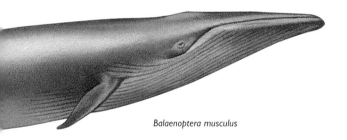

*Balaenoptera musculus*

# Fin Whale

The second largest living animal after the blue whale, the fin whale is among the fastest of whales, and while feeding, can attain bursts of speed of 19–25 miles (30–40 km) per hour. Like the blue whale, it is sexually mature at about 5 or 6 years, and probably lives in excess of 70–80 years. These superb mammals were hunted in the North Atlantic until as recently as 1989.

**Appearance** A distinctive asymmetrical color pattern is the most noticeable feature of this large, sleek, streamlined whale. Body color is generally a dark gray to brown on the back, with the throat, belly and undersides of the flippers and tail flukes being white. The head has an asymmetrical pigmentation: The right lower jaw is white, while the left is mostly dark. Baleen plates are creamy white for the first third of the right side; the rest are dark gray, often with yellow to cream stripes. A light gray "chevron" pattern occurs in most animals just behind the head.

**Reproduction** Gestation period is 11 months, and a single young is born mid-winter. Sexual maturity for Southern Hemisphere males is 62 feet (19 m), and

females 65½ feet (20 m). Northern Hemisphere whales are smaller: Males mature at 57–60 feet (17.4–18.3 m), and females at 60–62 feet (18.3–19 m).

**Comment** Because of its size and cosmopolitan presence, the fin whale was extensively whaled from the late 1800s in the North Atlantic, then in the North Pacific and the Southern oceans. By the 1930s fin whale catches had increased in the Southern Ocean. In the 1970s, seriously declining stocks were protected from whaling. Some whaling continued in the North Atlantic into the 1980s and indigenous whaling still occurs off Greenland.

## KEY FACTS

♀ 85 ft (26 m)

♂ 69 ft (21 m)

**Other names** Common rorqual, razorback, finn, finback
**Size at birth** 21 ft (6.4 m)
**Weight** 45–75 tonnes/tons
**Diet** Swarming euphausiids; some fish such as capelin and herring
**Group size** Groups of 6–10 animals; can also occur in pairs or single animals
**Habitat** Generally open ocean, can be seen near the coast; migration geared to season and food supply
**Distribution** From the tropics to polar waters, in all oceans

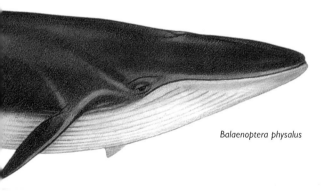

*Balaenoptera physalus*

# Sei Whale

The sei whale is one of five members of the genus *Balaenoptera* and one of six whales known as "rorquals." The word rorqual derives from an Old Norse word meaning "groove-throat." All the rorquals have a large number of throat pleats, which allow the gullet to expand and the whales to gulp down large quantities of water and prey through wide-opening jaws.

**Appearance** The sei whale is the middle whale in size among the five Balaenopterid rorquals. It looks like a typical rorqual, with the characteristic narrow snout; the erect, sickle-shaped dorsal fin; and the large, slender pectoral fins. The sei is dark gray and the body is slender and muscular. The color on the chin, throat and ventral surface appears pale, and there are mottled patches and scarring on the back and sides. This light-colored scarring can give the body a galvanized metallic look. The well-defined dorsal fin is about two-thirds of the way down the back. The rostrum is slightly arched and it has one prominent ridge from the tip of the rostrum to the blowhole, a feature that distinguishes it from its relative, Bryde's whale, which has three ridges. It is distinguished from its other close relative, the fin whale, by the symmetrical coloring on either side of its head.

*Balaenoptera borealis*

**Reproduction** A single young is born in mid-winter after a gestation period of about 11.5 months. The mother suckles the calf for about nine months. Sei whales from the Southern Hemisphere populations are slightly larger than those from the Northern Hemisphere. Both males and females are sexually mature at about between six and twelve years, and there is a calving interval of two to three years.

**Comment** Sei whales are rarely seen because of their preference for offshore waters. Most of what we know about them comes from studies associated with whaling or whaling management. Sei whales, which at one time became scarce, have probably increased in numbers in recent years because of whaling restrictions.

## KEY FACTS

♀ 56 ft (17 m)

♂ 50 ft (15 m)

**Other names** Japan finner, sardine whale, coalfish, pollack whale, short-headed sperm whale, lesser cachalot
**Size at birth** 15 ft (4.5 m)
**Weight** Average 20–25 tons/tonnes
**Diet** An opportunistic feeder, taking shoaling and swarming prey, such as copepods, fish, squid and krill
**Group size** Small pods of 3–5 individuals
**Habitat** Open ocean, rarely coastal; may follow oceanic temperature and current lines
**Distribution** Most oceans and seas, but rarely in polar areas

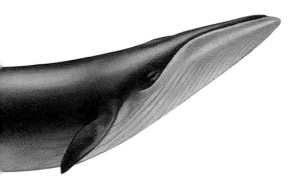

# BRYDE'S WHALE

The Bryde's whale is unique among baleen whales in that it spends the entire year in relatively infertile tropical and subtropical zones, where water temperatures are greater than 68°F (20°C) and does not migrate to cold-water feeding areas. The Bryde's whale is named after Mr. J. Bryde, who helped build the first whaling factory in Durban, South Africa.

**Appearance** Bryde's whale (which is pronounced *brood-ess*) is often confused with the sei whale, because it is quite similar in both size and appearance. However, the major difference is that Bryde's whale possesses three head ridges. In general, this whale is dark gray, with some white on the throat and chin. It has the classic rorqual head—narrow with a pointed snout and 40–50 throat grooves that enable the mouth to expand when feeding. The dorsal fin is well defined and sickle-shaped. It is positioned about two-thirds of the way down the back. Stocky in its appearance, this species has pointed, relatively short pectoral fins and 255–365 slate gray baleen plates up to 18 inches (46 cm) long in each side of the upper jaw.

**Reproduction** The existence of inshore and offshore forms of this species makes it difficult to define a particular breeding season. Calves are born after a 12-month gestation period, then probably suckled for about 6 months. Males can reproduce at 38–41 feet (11.6–12.4 m), females at 40–42 feet (12–12.8 m).

**Comment** Typical feeding behavior can be observed at two sites. In the Gulf of California, Mexico, these whales feed alone or in groups of up to about five. In Tosa Bay, Kochi Prefecture, Japan, the 15 or so resident whales feed alone or in mother–calf pairs. In both areas, the whales often approach whale-watch boats.

### KEY FACTS

♀ 51 ft (15.6 m)

♂ 45 ft (13.7 m)

**Other names** None
**Size at birth** 10–13 ft (3–4 m)
**Weight** 16–18 tons/tonnes
**Diet** Generally larger size prey, often shoaling fish species; will also feed on krill
**Group size** Over a few square miles, aggregations of 10–23 can be seen; mostly found alone or in pairs
**Habitat** Some resident inshore animals, others offshore and migratory. All prefer warm waters above 68°F (20°C)
**Distribution** Worldwide in tropical and subtropical oceans

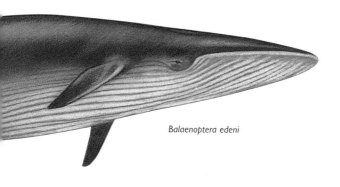

*Balaenoptera edeni*

143

# HUMPBACK WHALE

Stockier in shape and a much slower swimmer than the other rorquals, the humpback is nevertheless an agile and acrobatic performer and a favorite of whale-watchers. Herman Melville, author of *Moby Dick*, described it as "the most gamesome and light-hearted of all the whales." The humpback is also noted for its song, longer and far more complex than that of other whales.

**Appearance** Highly visible, and probably the most familiar of the large whales, the humpback occasionally breaches spectacularly. Some aspects of the humpback's anatomy set it apart from other rorquals. It has a stout black and white body and the extremely long pectoral fins generally have white undersides. The dorsal flukes are large, and the undersides have a mixed pattern of black and white. As with other rorquals, the ventral area, from the chin to the abdomen, contains a series of grooves or pleats that allow the throat to expand during feeding. Compared to the slim, sleek classic rorquals, the humpback is bulkier. The skin of the head is knobby and often covered in barnacles. The dorsal fin may be reduced to a fleshy hump.

**Reproduction** Young are born in warm waters during late fall and winter after an extensive migration. Gestation period is 11–11.5 months. Sexual maturity in males is reached at 38 feet (11.5 m), and in females at 40 feet (12 m)—at about five years.

**Comment** Humpbacks usually lift their flukes before a deep dive. The flukes have a distinctive pattern on the underside, which varies from almost white with black markings to almost black with only a few white markings. These marking often allow the identification of individual humpback whales.

*Megaptera novaeangliae*

**KEY FACTS**

♀ 45 ft (13.7 m)

♂ 42 ft (12.9 m)

**Other names** *Baleine à bosse* in French, *rorcual jorobado* in Spanish
**Size at birth** Average 14 ft (4.3 m)
**Weight** 25–30 tons/tonnes
**Diet** Krill, generally euphausiids; also some schooling fish, such as mackerel or herring
**Group size** 1–3 for migrating; larger groups when feeding or breeding
**Habitat** Breed in warm, shallow tropical waters, but migrate to polar regions for summer feeding
**Distribution** Widely distributed around the world

# MINKE WHALE

The minke whale was formerly called the little piked whale or little finner in some parts of the world. This slim, relatively small baleen whale is readily observed by whale-watchers. Most of the time, minkes on their feeding grounds feed steadily, taking little notice of people or boats. Occasionally, though, they exhibit curiosity, even swimming beside boats for up to 30 minutes.

**Appearance**  The smallest of the rorquals and the second smallest of the baleen whales, the minke whale is slightly larger than an orca. A streamlined and graceful animal, the minke has a pointed head and a single, prominent ridge from the tip of the upper jaw to the blowholes. Its tall, sickle-shaped dorsal fin is about two-thirds of the way down the back. Generally a dark slate gray, the color changes to a paler gray or white on the belly. Some shading occurs on the sides, and in some animals, particularly in the Northern Hemisphere, a prominent white band can be found across each flipper. Behind the head, there may also be a paler area that resembles a small cape. Minkes have 50–70 throat grooves and 230–360 creamy baleen plates on each side of the upper jaw.

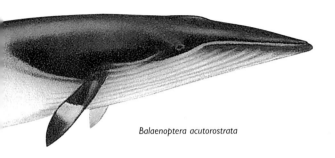

*Balaenoptera acutorostrata*

♀ 33 ft (10 m)

♂ 26 ft (8 m)

**Other names** Lesser rorqual, pikehead
**Size at birth** 8–9 ft (2.4–2.8 m)
**Weight** 8–13 tons/tonnes
**Diet** Preferred prey is krill; also fish, and occasionally small mollusks
**Group size** Generally solitary or groups of 2–3; larger aggregations when feeding
**Habitat** Generally open ocean; can be found near the ice edge in polar areas
**Distribution** Worldwide, with populations in the Southern Hemisphere and the North Pacific and North Atlantic oceans

**Reproduction** Mating probably occurs in late winter. A single young is born in low-latitude waters, after a 10-month gestation period. At sexual maturity, Southern Hemisphere whales are larger than Northern Hemisphere ones. The average length is 23 feet (7 m) for males, 24 feet (7.3 m) for females.

**Comment** The minke whale is the most abundant of the rorquals and is found in all the world's oceans. It is the only baleen whale that is still being regularly hunted by commercial whalers. Estimates of its population size are therefore controversial and varied. They range from 500,000 to 1,000,000 individuals worldwide.

# TOOTHED WHALES

Toothed whales live in a variety of habitats, from harbors, shorelines and coastal rivers to the deep sea. The most familiar group, the dolphins, belongs to the family that claims the greatest number of species. They are noted for the variety of their vivid skin patterns. From the bulky sperm whales to the delicate porpoises, toothed whales differ greatly from each other in size and shape. They also vary in the number and kind of teeth they possess: At one extreme is the male narwhal, which has only two teeth, both in the upper jaw, and one of which grows outward as a tusk; at the other are some oceanic dolphins, which have hundreds of cone-shaped teeth distributed between both jaws.

## SPERM WHALE

In many ways, the sperm whale can claim the title "lord of the sea." It ranges throughout all the world's oceans, except the high Arctic; it has the largest brain of any animal; and it is the largest of the toothed whales, growing in some cases to more than 65 feet (20 m) long. It seems fitting that Herman Melville chose the sperm whale as the protagonist for his famous novel, *Moby Dick*.

**Appearance** This, the largest of the toothed whales, has a characteristic, unmistakable body shape unlike that of any other whale. The massive rectangular head can, in adults, constitute one-third of its total body length. There is a single, S-shaped blowhole on the left side of the forehead and the long, narrow lower jaw fits neatly into the underside of the head. The overall color is dark brown, gray or occasionally black, and there is a light gray ventral patch. Older animals, especially males, often bear scars on the head resulting from fights with other males, and there may also be sucker marks of large squid. The 50 large conical teeth are arranged in parallel rows on both sides of the lower jaw.

**Reproduction** This is a slow-breeding species with calves born in summer and fall after a gestation period of 14–15 months.

Males grow much larger and heavier than females. Females can reproduce at about 26–29½ feet (8–9 m); males when they are 36–39 feet (11–12 m) long.

**Comment** Although they have never been witnessed by humans, the fierce battles fought between sperm whales and giant squid, which are an important part of this whale's diet, are the stuff of legend. Scars on the body of sperm whales, and the beak of giant squid found in the stomach of dead sperm whales, provide compelling evidence of these violent encounters.

### KEY FACTS

♂ 65 1/2 ft (20 m)

♀ 43 ft (13 m)

**Other names** Cachalot, short-headed sperm whale
**Size at birth** 13 ft (4 m)
**Weight** Ranges from ♂ 45 tons/tonnes to ♀ 20 tons/tonnes
**Diet** Almost exclusively cephalopods (squid and octopus)
**Group size** Family groups of 10–20
**Habitat** Oceanic; prefers deep waters, especially around seamounts and continental shelf edges
**Distribution** All oceans, females and young prefer water above 59°F (15°C); adult males also inhabit polar waters

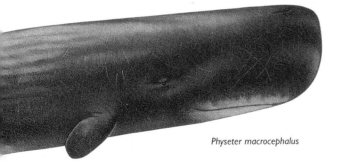

*Physeter macrocephalus*

# Pygmy Sperm Whale

Little is known of the pygmy sperm whale, or its relative, the dwarf sperm whale. Although it has a definite dorsal fin, its small size, slow movements and indistinct blow make it hard to sight. Even when sighted this whale can be difficult to identify positively, except during rest periods, when it floats at the surface, its head and back exposed and only its tail hanging limply in the water.

**Appearance** A sharklike head, false gill markings and underslung lower jaw make this small, robust whale look like a fish at first glance. The short, narrow mouth under the head has 12–16 curved, needle-shaped teeth on each side of the lower jaw. In adults, the head takes on a rectangular shape. Viewed from above, the dorsal surface of the body is dark bluish gray. The ventral surface is a paler, often slightly pinkish, color. A small sickle-shaped dorsal fin is located behind the mid-point of the back. The pectoral fins are relatively large and slightly rounded and the flukes are large and tapered.

**Reproduction** The little we know about this whale's reproduction comes from stranded animals. Calving is probably annual, and the gestation period is about 11 months. Sexual maturity is reached at 9–10 feet (2.7–3 m).

**Comment** A warm-water, offshore species, these whales frequently strand on beaches, especially in South Africa, New Zealand, southeastern Australia and on the east coast of North America. Though they are rarely seen in the wild, whale-watch tours off Dominica have encountered them in recent years. They seem to be shy animals, seldom approaching boats. When frightened, they may release brown fecal material that clouds the water and may work as a decoy, like squid ink.

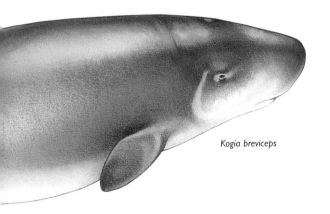

*Kogia breviceps*

## KEY FACTS

♂♀ 10¹/₂ ft (3.3 m)

**Other names** None
**Size at birth** 4 ft (1.2 m)
**Weight** 900 lb (400 kg)
**Diet** Primarily oceanic squid; some small numbers of fish and deep-sea shrimp
**Group size** Small groups of fewer than 5 individuals; a difficult species to observe at sea, but frequently found stranded
**Habitat** Oceanic; tends to stay close to or over the continental slope
**Distribution** Probably occurs in widely distributed areas, including temperate, subtropical and tropical seas

## BAIRD'S BEAKED WHALE

Although the Japanese had long been catching it with hand harpoons, Baird's beaked whale was not classified until 1882, when researcher Leonhard Stejneger picked up a four-toothed skull on Bering Island. The following year he published his discovery, honoring his colleague, Spencer Baird, the newly appointed Secretary of the Smithsonian Institution, with the species name.

**Appearance** The largest member of its family—it is several times as long as some other beaked whales—Baird's beaked whale is an impressive animal, with a long, well-defined beak and a bulging forehead. The lower jaw is longer than the upper jaw, making the front pair of teeth clearly visible, even when the mouth is closed. There is another pair of slightly smaller teeth farther back in the lower jaw. The relatively slender body is a uniform brownish gray, with a pattern of scratches and marks that become more numerous as the animal ages. The underside, especially around the throat, is often covered with irregular blotches of white.

**Reproduction** The peak season for calving is March–April, and the estimated gestation period is 17 months. Sexual maturity is

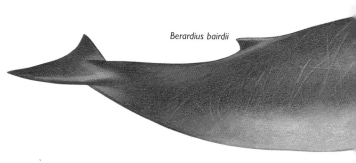

*Berardius bairdii*

reached at about 8–10 years—when females are about 34½ feet (10.5 m) and males about 33 feet (10 m) long.

**Comment** Baird's beaked whales are social animals, and stay in tight groups, ranging in number from 3 to 30 or more individuals. Like other beaked whales, Baird's beaked whales dive deeply. Dive times can be as long as 67 minutes, although 25 to 35 minutes is more common. The scarring on their back indicates that there is probably a great deal of play or aggression within groups of these whales.

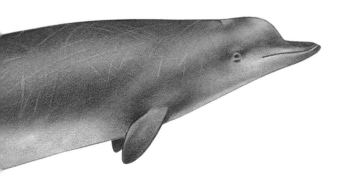

**KEY FACTS**

♀ 42 ft (12.8 m)

♂ 39 ft (11.9 m)

**Other names** Bottlenose whale; in Japan it is called *tsuchi-kujira* or *tsuchimbo*
**Size at birth** 15 ft (4.5 m)
**Weight** 11–12 tons/tonnes
**Diet** Mostly bottom-dwelling organisms, such as squid, skate, and crustaceans
**Group size** Often up to 50
**Habitat** Generally restricted to above the continental slope and oceanic seamounts
**Distribution** North Pacific Ocean (including California), and the Japan, Okhotsk and Bering seas

# CUVIER'S BEAKED WHALE

One of the most abundant and widespread beaked whales in the world, Cuvier's, along with Baird's beaked whale and the northern bottlenose whale, is one of the three most watched beaked species. It is difficult to predict sightings, but Cuvier's beaked whales are sometimes seen on the whale-watch trips in the Mediterranean, Hawaii, the Canary Islands and off South America.

**Appearance** Cuvier's beaked whale has a pair of V-shaped throat grooves and a slightly upturned mouthline. Its small beak appears continuous with the melon. A small, falcate dorsal fin is set about two-thirds of the way along the back. The pigmentation pattern varies from one individual to another, probably reflecting geographical race or age. Males lighten as they grow older; the head and nape eventually change from a gray-brown to white.

General body color can be acorn brown, tan, light brown, or gun-metal blue. The two conical teeth in the front of the lower jaw erupt only in the males.

**Reproduction** Females can reach sexual maturity at 16½ feet (5.1 m), but most may be longer than this. Males are probably longer—18 feet (5.5 m) or even

more—at sexual maturity. The season of birth and gestation period are unknown.

**Comment** The first details of this species were published in 1823, when the French anatomist Georges Cuvier created a new genus and described what he thought to be an extinct whale. In the 1870s it was realized that Cuvier's fossil represented a living species, and numerous disparate beaked whale findings from all over the world were re-identified as Cuvier's beaked whales.

*Ziphius cavirostris*

## KEY FACTS

♀ 24½ ft (7.5 m)

♂ 23 ft (7 m)

**Other names** Goose-beaked whale
**Size at birth** About 9 ft (2.75 m)
**Weight** 3 tons/tonnes
**Diet** Principally squid and deep-sea fish
**Group size** Occurs singly or in groups of 2–7 individuals
**Habitat** A deepwater animal; rarely seen near the coast
**Distribution** A widely distributed and probably common species, found in all seas except polar waters

# NORTHERN BOTTLENOSE WHALE

Both sexes of this species regularly approach ships, and this has made them more likely to be hunted, studied, and, more recently, whale-watched than the other beaked whales. Many researchers have watched them playing and socializing. Long-term relationships have been observed among northern bottlenose whales of the same sex, but not among mixed sexes.

**Appearance** A distinctive head shape gives this species its common name. It has a prominent, squarish melon (most notable in the males) and a long, tubelike snout. The dorsal fin is small, sickle-shaped, and set well back on the body. There is little color variation over the body, which is dark grayish brown on the back, changing to a lighter shade on the belly. Some individuals also develop a rather blotchy appearance, and the head area, in particular, gradually becomes paler. There are two conical teeth in the tip of the lower jaw, which erupt only in males. There may also be 10–20 vestigial teeth in the gums of the upper and lower jaws.

**Reproduction** On average, males are 24½ feet (7.5 m) when sexually mature; females are slightly shorter at 22½ feet

(6.9 m). Calves are born in April–June after a gestation period of about 12 months.

**Comment** These whales have been hunted more than any other beaked whale. In the late nineteenth century, Scottish whalers used to call old northern bottlenose bulls "flatheads." Tens of thousands have been killed since then. Scientists disagree about the extent to which the species has been depleted, and about its current status.

*Hyperoodon ampullatus*

## KEY FACTS

♂ 32 ft (9.8 m)

♀ 28½ ft (8.7 m)

**Other names** *Andehval* (Norwegian), *butskopf* (German)
**Size at birth** 11½ feet (3.5m)
**Weight** Estimated at several tons
**Diet** Specialist squid feeder; also sea cucumbers, sea stars and prawns
**Group size** Pod size usually 4–10; several groups often in one area
**Habitat** Deep waters of 28–63°F (-2–17°C) on the continental shelf edge and slopes
**Distribution** North Atlantic—west from New England to Greenland, and east from the Straits of Gibraltar to Svalbard

# NARWHAL

The narwhal's tusk. which is really a tooth, may be the source of the unicorn myths. Narwhals have two teeth, in the upper jaw. In females they rarely erupt. In males, the left tooth erupts, penetrating the upper beak and spiraling out. The tusk is mainly for display and is used to compete for females. Tusked narwhals are unmistakable. Calves and females may be confused with belugas.

**Appearance** The narwhal male's most prominant feature is its conspicuous tusk, a modified tooth that reaches a length of about 6½ feet (2 m). Many other features vary with age—most notably the tail flukes, which change shape as the animal grows, gradually becoming semicircular, with the curve on the trailing edges. There is no dorsal fin, and the body is stocky with short pectoral fins. Color also varies: Calves are a uniform gray but later

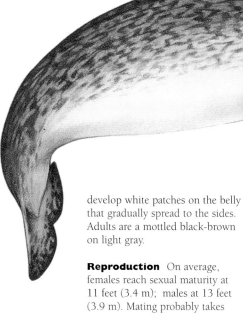

develop white patches on the belly that gradually spread to the sides. Adults are a mottled black-brown on light gray.

**Reproduction** On average, females reach sexual maturity at 11 feet (3.4 m); males at 13 feet (3.9 m). Mating probably takes

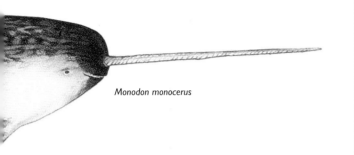

*Monodon monocerus*

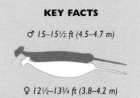

## KEY FACTS

♂ 15–15½ ft (4.5–4.7 m)

♀ 12½–13¾ ft (3.8–4.2 m)

**Other names** *Kelleluak, kakortok, quilalugaq* (Inuit)
**Size at birth** 5 ft (1.6 m)
**Weight** 1.6 tons/tonnes
**Diet** Squid and shrimp; some fish, such as Arctic cod
**Group size** Immediate group 2–10; pods can be thousands in a large area
**Habitat** Deep fiords in Arctic and subarctic waters; generally near ice
**Distribution** Above Arctic Circle, from central Canadian Arctic to Greenland and to the central Russian Arctic; sometimes migration between areas occurs

place in the arctic spring, and there is a gestation period of about 14–15 months. Calves are born at the height of summer in July– August. Female narwhals give birth approximately every three years. The tusks begin to erupt in young males when they are about one year old.

**Comment** The narwhal and the beluga are the sole members of the family of "white whales" (Monodontidae), which are considered whales by some and dolphins by others. They have many characteristics of larger dolphins, but also qualify as a separate family of toothed whales.

# BELUGA

Sometimes called the white whale, the beluga, with its all-white, sometimes yellowish, body is one of the most distinctive of whales, although with its low profile and habit of leaping only rarely, it can be difficult to locate at sea. The beluga is also one of the most vocal of all cetaceans. Its sounds can often be heard clearly above water or through the hull of a boat.

**Appearance** The young of this fairly small, almost pure ivory or white, whale are a dark brownish gray. This gradually fades, and all animals are light-colored by the time they are 5–12 years old. The beluga has a small, bulbous head, very short beak, a robust body, a small dorsal ridge instead of a dorsal fin, and small rounded pectoral fins. The flukes are large and rounded, with convex trailing edges. The teeth are conical; there are nine in each side of the upper jaw and eight in each side of the lower jaw. These can be decidedly worn in older animals. Because their vertebrae are unfused, belugas have a relatively flexible neck.

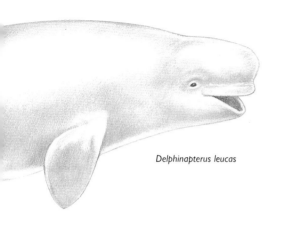

*Delphinapterus leucas*

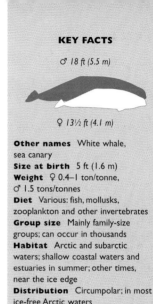

**KEY FACTS**

♂ 18 ft (5.5 m)

♀ 13½ ft (4.1 m)

**Other names** White whale, sea canary
**Size at birth** 5 ft (1.6 m)
**Weight** ♀ 0.4–1 ton/tonne, ♂ 1.5 tons/tonnes
**Diet** Various: fish, mollusks, zooplankton and other invertebrates
**Group size** Mainly family-size groups; can occur in thousands
**Habitat** Arctic and subarctic waters; shallow coastal waters and estuaries in summer; other times, near the ice edge
**Distribution** Circumpolar; in most ice-free Arctic waters

**Reproduction** Females reach sexual maturity when they are at least five years of age, or later; males at about eight years of age. The mating season varies: In some areas it is late winter or spring; other populations mate in May. Gestation lasts for about 14–14.5 months, and calves are born in spring or summer.

**Comment** Large groups have been known to swim hundreds of miles up rivers in Russia, Canada and northern Europe. They have little fear of shallow waters, and if stranded are often able to wait and refloat on the next tide. Belugas have been hunted for centuries. However, pollution seems to pose a greater threat to their survival.

# FALSE KILLER WHALE

The false killer whale, sometimes also called "pseudorca," is a warm-water resident of the world's oceans. Like orcas and pilot whales, it has a complex social nature. But with its fast, acrobatic swimming, it is often more like a playful, inquisitive dolphin than a pilot whale or orca. These whales often breach, sometimes landing on their sides or back with a great splash.

**Appearance** The upright dorsal fin of this slim, medium-size whale is slightly rounded at the tip, and located midway along the back. The head has a rounded snout, which overhangs the lower jaw. There are 7–12 pairs of conical teeth in each of the upper and lower jaws. General body color is black, with lighter areas on the chest and head. The S-shaped pectoral fins are quite distinctive; each has a broad hump on the leading edge.

**Reproduction** Breeds year-round. Estimated gestation period varies from 12 to 15.5 months. Body lengths at sexual maturity also vary, which may indicate the existence of different populations. In males, the length ranges from 13 to 15 feet (3.9–4.5 m), and in females from 12 to 14 feet

(3.6–4.2 m). Mass-stranded whales have provided most of what we know about the reproductive biology of this species.

**Comment** False killers are hunted off China and Japan and in the Caribbean, and they are also sometimes killed accidentally in fish nets, including tuna purse-seines and pelagic gill nets. They have a reputation for stealing fish off lines and from nets. They have also been reported to attack dolphins escaping from tuna nets and there is one report of their attacking and killing a humpback whale calf near Hawaii.

*Pseudorca crassidens*

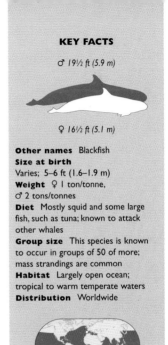

**KEY FACTS**

♂ 19½ ft (5.9 m)

♀ 16½ ft (5.1 m)

**Other names** Blackfish
**Size at birth**
Varies; 5–6 ft (1.6–1.9 m)
**Weight** ♀ 1 ton/tonne,
♂ 2 tons/tonnes
**Diet** Mostly squid and some large fish, such as tuna; known to attack other whales
**Group size** This species is known to occur in groups of 50 of more; mass strandings are common
**Habitat** Largely open ocean; tropical to warm temperate waters
**Distribution** Worldwide

165

# ORCA

The largest of all dolphins, the orca is found in all seas and is one of the most widely distributed animals on Earth. Until recently, it had the reputation of a fierce killer. As top predator in the sea, the orca's diet extends to several hundred known species—a more diverse and extensive diet than that of any other whale or dolphin. There is no known case of an orca ever killing a human.

## Appearance

This large toothed whale has a very tall dorsal fin—much taller and more upright in males than in females—a rounded head, a blunt snout and a robust body boldly marked in glossy black and white. The pectoral fins are large and paddle-like and, in the males, can grow up to 6½ feet (2 m) long. The flukes are broad with a deep central notch. The pectoral fins and dorsal surface of the tail flukes are black, as is most of the back.

White occurs on the ventral surface from the lower jaw to the urinogenital area, and there is also a large patch of white above and behind each eye. Each side of the upper and lower jaws bears 10–12 large, recurved teeth.

**Reproduction**  Males are about 19 feet (5.8 m) long when they reach sexual maturity; females are about 16 feet (4.9 m). Gestation

period is thought to be 12–16 months, with most calves born between October and March.

**Comment** A 25-year study off British Columbia and Washington State has found that orcas stay in long-term social groups, or pods, for life—an average of 29 years for males and 50 years for females. Residents live in close family pods of up to 50 and subsist on fish; transient pods of between one and seven feed on marine mammals. The two groups do not mix with each other.

*Orcinus orca*

### KEY FACTS

♂ 32 ft (9.75 m)

♀ 28 ft (8.5 m)

**Other names** Killer whale, blackfish, grampus
**Size at birth** 6½–8 ft (2–2.5 m)
**Weight** ♀ 7.5 tons/tonnes,
♂ 10.5 tons/tonnes
**Diet** Diverse; often other marine mammals, including large whales; also fish, birds and even turtles
**Group size** Stable pods of 3–25
**Habitat** Ranges from coastal to open sea; from equator to polar areas
**Distribution** Occurs in all oceans and seas

# SHORT-BEAKED COMMON DOLPHIN

Over the years, more than 20 species of common dolphins have been proposed and discarded, but until recently only one was officially recognized. In 1994, a new species was created by splitting the original common dolphin into long-beaked and short-beaked species. The short-beaked common dolphin kept the original scientific name, *Delphinus delphis*, and the new species took a new name, *D. capensis*. However, even within the two species, there is little variation.

**Appearance**  The common dolphin is slender and stream-lined. Its long beak is separated from the melon by a distinct crease. The color pattern is striking, with a dark brown to black dorsal surface, including appendages, and a white ventral surface. This is offset by yellow front flank patches, and light gray rear flanks and tail stock. A narrow dark stripe runs forward from the black eye surround to the front of the melon. Striping also occurs between the chin and flippers. Each side of each jaw has 80–100 small pointed teeth.

*Delphinus delphis*

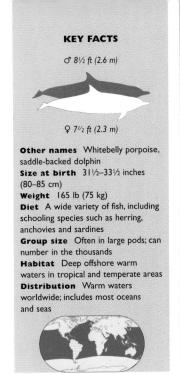

**KEY FACTS**

♂ 8½ ft (2.6 m)

♀ 7½ ft (2.3 m)

**Other names**  Whitebelly porpoise, saddle-backed dolphin

**Size at birth**  31½–33½ inches (80–85 cm)

**Weight**  165 lb (75 kg)

**Diet**  A wide variety of fish, including schooling species such as herring, anchovies and sardines

**Group size**  Often in large pods; can number in the thousands

**Habitat**  Deep offshore warm waters in tropical and temperate areas

**Distribution**  Warm waters worldwide; includes most oceans and seas

**Reproduction**  A number of different populations and stocks may account for variations in both length at sexual maturity and breeding seasons. Females, on average, become sexually mature at about 6 feet (1.8 m); males at 6½ feet (2 m). Gestation period is 11–12 months and births occur all year round.

**Comment**  Common dolphins travel in groups of 10 to 500 in most areas, with up to 2,000 or more in the eastern tropical Pacific. They are so acrobatic and boisterous that the noise of their approach can often be picked up from miles away. Their high-pitched sounds can sometimes be heard as they bow ride.

# PANTROPICAL SPOTTED DOLPHIN

Often called "spotters," or simply spotted
dolphins, pantropical spotted dolphins are a
delightful sighting on any marine nature tour.
They travel with ships, charging to the bow or
the stern to ride the waves and making long, low
leaps clear of the water as they swim along. Their
breaches are high and frequent, if a little less
acrobatic than those of the long-snouted spinner
dolphin. In the eastern Pacific alone, there are
at least two main forms within the pantropical
species—one coastal, the other offshore. The
coastal species is larger and more robust, with
a thicker beak and more spots.

*Stenella attenuata*

**Appearance** The pantropical
spotted dolphin is a slender
animal. The extent of the white
spotting depends on the age
and/or geographical region of
the individual. Spots appear after
birth, and become bigger and
more numerous with age. An
overall dark gray background

forms a cape-like pattern from the
top of the head to halfway down
the animal then sweeps up behind
the hooked dorsal fin. The ventral
surface is a lighter gray. There are
35–48 small teeth on each side of
the upper jaw and 34–47 on each
side of the lower jaw.

### KEY FACTS

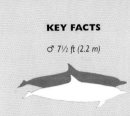

♂ 7½ ft (2.2 m)

♀ 6¾ ft (2.1 m)

**Other names** Spotted dolphin
**Size at birth** 34 in (87 cm)
**Weight** 262 lb (119 kg)
**Diet** A surface-water feeder, takes squid and flying fish
**Group size** Large variation in school size, from a few individuals to thousands
**Habitat** Tropical oceans with warm surface temperatures
**Distribution** In a band each side of the equator, varying in latitude from 25°N to 15°S off South America, and from 40°N to 40°S in the Atlantic

**Reproduction** The gestation period of 11–12 months indicates that mating and calving probably occur at the same time of year. The season depends on location of the group, usually May and September. These animals are quite old and large when they begin to breed: about 12 years and 6½ feet (1.9 m) for males; 9 years and 6 feet (1.8 m) for females.

**Comment** Tuna purse-seine fishing, particularly in the eastern tropical Pacific, has seriously depleted numbers of these dolphins. Hundreds of thousands of dolphins were killed every year in the 1960s and 1970s, until conservation measures began to take effect in the late 1980s. Although not endangered, these dolphins still suffer some losses.

## LONG-SNOUTED SPINNER DOLPHIN

This dolphin is famous for its fantastic spinning leaps, in which it breaches high out of the water, then rolls on its longitudinal axis, making up to seven complete turns. Few, if any, dolphins leap as high or as often, and no others, except the closely related clymene dolphin, *Stenella clymene*, are known to spin. Spinner dolphins are frequently observed around Hawaii, Mexico and Japan.

**Appearance** The long-snouted spinner dolphin is a particularly slender dolphin with a long, thin beak. There are several distinct forms of the species, and individuals differ in some important features. The dorsal fin can vary from slightly sickle-shaped, particularly in older males, to erect and triangular. Spinners are generally an overall monotone gray; others are gray with a white belly. Still others show a three-part color pattern: gray cape, light gray sides and a white belly. Most spinner dolphins have dark stripes from the eyes to the pectoral fins, and dark lips and beak tip. They have 44–64 conical teeth on each side of the upper jaw and 42–62 on each side of the lower jaw.

*Stenella longirostris*

♂♀ 7 ft (2.1 m)

**Other names** Four distinct forms of *S. longirostris* are recognized

**Size at birth**
Average 30 in (77 cm)

**Weight** Average size 165 lb (75 kg)

**Diet** Prefers fish and squid found well below surface level

**Group size** As in other *Stenella* species, from a few animals to hundreds; some mixing of schools with other dolphins

**Habitat** Tropical and subtropical waters north and south of the equator

**Distribution** All oceans

**Reproduction** Most life history has been obtained from a single population. These dolphins reach sexual maturity when they are 5–5½ feet (1.6–1.7 m) long, and breed annually in late spring or early summer. A single young is born after a gestation period of 10–11 months.

**Comment** Because of its acrobatics, the spinner was one of the first dolphins to be captured for aquariums in the North Pacific, but it does not thrive in captivity. The main threat to spinners has come from tuna fisheries, which have caused the death of many hundreds of thousands. Even today their populations remain relatively depleted.

## FRASER'S DOLPHIN

In 1955, cetologist Francis Charles Fraser found a mislabeled skeleton in the British Museum. It had been collected 60 years earlier in Sarawak. He placed the specimen somewhere between *Delphinus*, the common dolphins, and *Lagenorhynchus*, the "lag" dolphins, so he invented an intermediate genus: *Lagenodelphis*, of which Fraser's dolphin is the only member.

**Appearance** Fraser's dolphin has a short but well-defined beak, a robust body, and short, pointed flippers and dorsal fin. Its most striking feature is the bold, dark gray striping: This occurs on the flippers and, especially, on the face and along the sides, giving the face a masked effect. The dark stripe is further accentuated by a cream border both above and below. The rest of the body is a dark brownish gray on the back and sides, and pink or white on the belly. As with many dolphin species, the patterns of the bands or stripes generally become more marked with age.

**Reproduction** Little is known about the reproductive behavior of this species. Females are thought to become sexually mature when they are about 7½ feet (2.3 m). Breeding season, weaning age and gestation period are unknown.

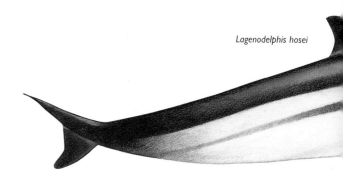

*Lagenodelphis hosei*

**Comment** These tropical, deepwater dolphins, which were first described in 1956, but not identified in the wild until the 1970s, can now be seen with some regularity on whale-watch trips. In some areas they avoid boats, but in South Africa they ride the bow waves and they have become a welcome feature of whale-watch tours in the Caribbean, the Philippines, Japan and other parts of the world. Fraser's dolphins often travel in groups of between 100 and 500 individuals, although occasionally they can be observed in groups of as many as 1,000. They sometimes associate or feed with other species of tropical toothed whales and dolphins.

## KEY FACTS

♂ ♀ 8½ ft (2.6 m)

**Other names** Originally called the sarawak dolphin
**Size at birth** About 3 ft (1 m)
**Weight** 440 lb (200 kg)
**Diet** Probably hunts at depths of more than 820 ft (250 m), taking a variety of fish, crustaceans and squid
**Group size** Pods can number 100 or more; often seen with other dolphin species
**Habitat** Offshore; encountered near coasts only around oceanic islands
**Distribution** Between latitudes 40°N and 40°S; a few sightings in Atlantic and Indian oceans

## WHITE-BEAKED DOLPHIN

The white-beaked dolphin shares most of its North Atlantic range with the Atlantic white-sided dolphin, but it ventures farther north into subarctic waters, making it the most northerly occurring of all dolphins. It is the most robust of all the "lag" dolphins (those belonging to the genus *Lagenorhynchus*) and has the thickest blubber layer. It is a powerful swimmer.

**Appearance** The white-beaked dolphin has a short, thick beak that is clearly separate from the melon, a robust body and a large sickle-shaped dorsal fin midway along its back. The overall color of the strongly patterned body is black to dark gray. There is white or light gray on the sides and dorsal surface of the tail stock, and forward of the dorsal fin. The undersides of the body are also white, and can sometimes appear mottled. The area between the eye and the flipper is often darkly spotted. Each half of each jaw contains 22–28 sharp teeth. Although larger and more robust, the white-beaked dolphin is frequently confused with the Atlantic white-sided dolphin.

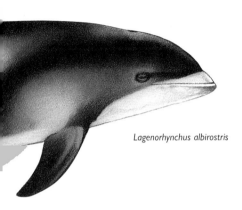

*Lagenorhynchus albirostris*

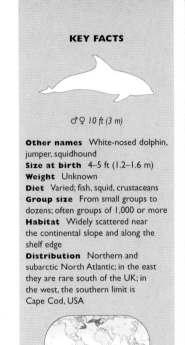

♂♀ 10 ft (3 m)

**Other names** White-nosed dolphin, jumper, squidhound
**Size at birth** 4–5 ft (1.2–1.6 m)
**Weight** Unknown
**Diet** Varied; fish, squid, crustaceans
**Group size** From small groups to dozens; often groups of 1,000 or more
**Habitat** Widely scattered near the continental slope and along the shelf edge
**Distribution** Northern and subarctic North Atlantic; in the east they are rare south of the UK; in the west, the southern limit is Cape Cod, USA

**Reproduction** Scientists have so far discovered extremely little about any aspect of this species' reproduction and life cycle, although most births tend to take place during the summer or in the early part of the fall.

**Comment** In spite of its name, the white-beaked dolphin's beak, when it can be seen in the wild, is often not white, but gray or even black. These animals tend to have white beaks towards the eastern end of their range.

177

# PACIFIC WHITE-SIDED DOLPHIN

This exclusively North Pacific dolphin acquired the species name *obliquidens*, meaning "slanting tooth," because of its slightly curved teeth. This feature was first noted by the fish taxonomist Theodore Nicholas Gill of the Smithsonian Institution, who gave the species its name after examining three skulls that had been collected near San Francisco.

**Appearance** A characteristic feature of the Pacific white-sided dolphin is its distinctive dorsal fin, which is tall, strongly recurved and bicolored. The front third of this fin is dark gray or black, and the rest a light gray. The small pectoral fins are similarly patterned. This animal's coloration is also distinctive. The relatively stocky body is grayish black on the back and paler gray on the sides, and a thin black line sharply demarcates a white belly. Pale streaking starts from the top of the head, just above the eye, and continues along the back to an enlarged gray patch on the sides of the tail stock. The beak is short and dark, which makes it difficult to detect, except at close quarters.

*Lagenorhynchus obliquidens*

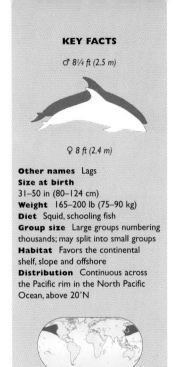

## KEY FACTS

♂ 8¼ ft (2.5 m)

♀ 8 ft (2.4 m)

**Other names** Lags
**Size at birth**
31–50 in (80–124 cm)
**Weight** 165–200 lb (75–90 kg)
**Diet** Squid, schooling fish
**Group size** Large groups numbering thousands; may split into small groups
**Habitat** Favors the continental shelf, slope and offshore
**Distribution** Continuous across the Pacific rim in the North Pacific Ocean, above 20°N

**Reproduction** Both males and females are sexually mature when they are 5½–7 feet (1.7–2.2 m) long. Calving and mating both take place from spring through to fall. Young are born after a gestation period of 10–12 months.

**Comment** This dolphin is very acrobatic and sociable. Its sociable nature extends beyond its species to other cetaceans, particularly northern right whale dolphins. It is intensely curious and will sometimes closely inspect boats.

# INDO-PACIFIC HUMP-BACKED DOLPHIN

This dolphin can often be identified purely by its surfacing behavior: The long beak appears first above the water and then the animal arches its back and appears to pause—unlike the surfacing behavior in other dolphins—before either dipping below or flipping its tail and diving. The taxonomy of this species is still being argued; there may be two species, one of them lacking the humpback for which the animal is named.

**Appearance** A highly variable species, the Indo-Pacific hump-backed dolphin is superficially similar to the bottlenose dolphin. It has a robust body and elongated snout or beak. It is so-named because its sickle-shaped dorsal fin sits on a distinct hump, or ridge, midway along the back, although this hump is obvious only in animals in the west of the range (west of Sumatra, Indonesia). Animals in the east and south of the range have a more prominent dorsal fin, but no distinctive hump. There is also a ridge, or keel, above and below the tail stock. Color pattern varies with age and population: In some areas, adults are an overall dark gray, leadlike color, and the young are lighter gray; in other regions, adults are very pale, almost white. The number of teeth in each side of the upper and lower jaws varies between 27 and 38.

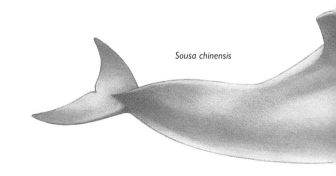

*Sousa chinensis*

**Reproduction** Very little is known. The breeding season is probably protracted, with a peak in summer. Only two sexually mature animals, both from South Africa, have been measured. They were an 8 foot (2.5 m) female, and a male measuring 9 feet (2.8 m).

**Comment** Indo-Pacific hump-backed dolphins often swim with other dolphins, mainly bottlenose, but also spinner dolphins and finless porpoises. They rarely bow ride or approach boats.

**KEY FACTS**

♂ 10½ ft (3.2 m)

♀ 8 ft (2.5 m)

**Other names**
*Parampuan laut* in Malaya
**Size at birth** About 3 ft (1 m)
**Weight** 625 lb (285 kg)
**Diet** Schooling fish such as mullet, sea bream and grunts
**Group size** Groups of 5–7 animals; occasionally form larger groups
**Habitat** Mangrove channels and shallow water less than 65½ ft (20 m) deep; will enter rivers and estuaries
**Distribution** Northern Australia; southern China; Indonesia; coastal Indian Ocean to South Africa

## BOTTLENOSE DOLPHIN

The bottlenose dolphin is the archetypal dolphin, found around the world, from cooler temperate to tropical waters. It lives both inshore and offshore, and is the active dolphin that leaps, bow rides, bodysurfs, splashes its tail and approaches boats and swimmers more than any other dolphin. The lone, sociable dolphins that have mixed with humans over the years, such as Fungie in Ireland and the dolphins of *Flipper* fame, are also mainly members of this species.

**Appearance** The bottlenose is a relatively large and robust dolphin. It has a well-formed melon, which is separated from the stocky snout by a marked crease. The dorsal fin, located near the middle of the back, is broad and triangular. The belly is off-white, and the sides of the head and body are a light gray, which gradually becomes deeper until it forms a dark bluish gray cape on the back. Striping occurs

from the melon to the eyes, and also from the eyes to the flipper. As they get older, these dolphins develop a white tip on the snout.

**Reproduction** This species undergoes a long adolescence: Females do not begin to breed until they are 9–10 years old;

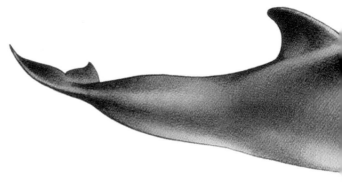

males when they reach 10–13 years. Gestation lasts for about 12 months; a single young is born in spring or summer.

**Comment** The food habits and hunting behavior of bottlenose dolphins vary greatly. They adapt their behavior to local conditions and circumstances, and only orcas eat a greater variety of food. Cooperative feeding occurs in South Carolina and Baja California, where dolphins chase fish on to the shore, then roll up on the beaches to grab them.

**KEY FACTS**

♂ 13 ft (4 m)

♀ 11¾ ft (3.6 m)

**Other names** Gray or black dolphin in North America; bottlenosed porpoise (erroneously)
**Size at birth** 3–4½ ft (1–1.3 m)
**Weight** 200–1,430 lb (90–650 kg)
**Diet** Inshore: fish, squid and octopus; offshore: bottom-dwelling and schooling fish and squid
**Group size** Up to 100 inshore to several hundred in oceanic groups
**Habitat** Wide variety: bays and lagoons in coastal areas; open ocean
**Distribution** Widely distributed from tropical to temperate seas

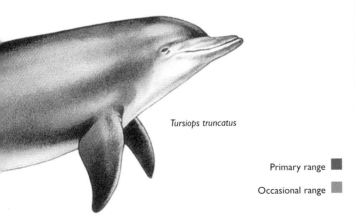

*Tursiops truncatus*

Primary range ■

Occasional range ■

# IRRAWADDY DOLPHIN

Named after the Irrawaddy River of Myanmar (formerly Burma), this dolphin has many attributes that put it in the family of oceanic dolphins, but some researchers consider it close to the beluga family. In the wild it can be confused with the finless porpoise, which is, however, much smaller and has no dorsal fin. From a distance, it may even sometimes be confused with a dugong.

**Appearance** With its blunt, rounded head, lack of a beak, and pale body color, the Irrawaddy dolphin resembles the beluga whale. However, while the beluga gradually turns white, the Irrawaddy dolphin remains gray— darker above, and paler below. It also possesses a small dorsal fin, which lies behind the midpoint of the body. Some unfused neck vertebrae allow the head free movement. The pectoral fins are quite large, with curved leading edges. There are 17–20 peglike teeth in each tooth row of the upper jaw, and 15–18 in each row of the lower jaw.

**Reproduction** Many aspects of the life history of this species are poorly understood. What little we

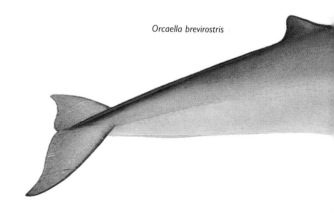

*Orcaella brevirostris*

do know has been obtained from captive animals. The evidence suggests that mating occurs in spring and early summer. Gestation period seems to be about 14 months.

**Comment** The Irrawaddy is often killed accidentally in shark gill nets in Australia as well as in fish traps and other nets within its range. But more serious threats to this dolphin arise from the destruction and degradation of its habitat by riverbank development and the construction of dams.

**KEY FACTS**

♂ 9 ft (2.7 m)

♀ 7½ ft (2.3 m)

**Other names** Pesut, lumbalumba
**Size at birth** About 3 ft (1 m)
**Weight** 200–330 lb (90–150 kg)
**Diet** Crustaceans and other invertebrates; also fish
**Group size** Generally small groups up to 6; groups of 15 have been observed
**Habitat** Found only in warm waters of the tropics and subtropics; prefers rivers and shallow coastal areas
**Distribution** South-East Asia and northern Australia; the range of this species is, as yet, not fully known

# Risso's Dolphin

Larger than any other cetacean that carries the name "dolphin," this easily recognized animal is sometimes informally grouped with the pilot whale, orca, false killer whale and other members of the family Delphinidae because of its size and blunt head. Compared to other cetaceans, Risso's dolphins have been little studied and not much is known about their status.

*Grampus griseus*

**Appearance** Adult Risso's dolphins are easily recognized by the extensive white scarring and blotching that covers what is otherwise a gray body. These scratches and blotches increase as the animals age and can sometimes become so extensive that some animals, especially older ones, appear almost white. The pectoral fins and the high, sickle-shaped dorsal fin are generally a darker shade of gray than the rest of the body, and there is an anchor-shaped white chest patch. A robust-looking dolphin, it has a large, blunt head and no beak, which gives it a somewhat squarish profile. The pectoral fins are long and sickle-shaped with pointed tips and the flukes are wide and pointed.

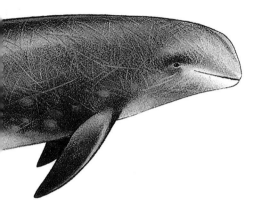

**KEY FACTS**

♂ 12½ ft (3.8 m)

♀ 10¾ ft (3.3 m)

**Other names** Grampus, gray grampus
**Size at birth** 4–5 ft (1.2–1.5 m)
**Weight** 880–1,100 lb (400–500 kg)
**Diet** Largely squid; some fish
**Group size** Groups up to 12; also sighted in pods numbering thousands; often with other dolphin species
**Habitat** Deep water
**Distribution** Tropical and warm temperate waters; avoids polar oceans; northern limits are Newfoundland and Shetland, the Gulf of Alaska and the northern Indian Ocean

**Reproduction** Both sexes become sexually mature at about 8½ feet (2.6 m) long. Young are born after a gestation period of 13–14 months. Calving generally occurs in summer, although there is some variation among the different populations.

**Comment** Some of the scars on these dolphins come from the teeth of other Risso's dolphins, possibly playing or fighting with each other. It also seems likely that some of the scarring comes from squid bites. These dolphins have a preference for squid.

187

# HECTOR'S DOLPHIN

New Zealand's own dolphin, the Hector's dolphin is one of the smallest cetaceans. Moving in small groups in the waters around New Zealand, these animals surface frequently to breathe, but they show little of their stout bodies. Although they are easy to miss because of their low profile and small size, they are easily identifiable by their characteristic rounded dorsal fin.

**Appearance** Typical of its genus, Hector's dolphin is a small, stocky animal with a blunt head and a low, rounded dorsal fin. The complex color combinations of black, white and gray give this species its distinctive appearance. Most of the torso is gray, with black on the tail, dorsal fin, side of the head around and back from the eye and tip of the lower jaw. White appears largely on the ventral surface, extending from the lower jaw back along the throat, belly, and part of the flank. There is also a white patch behind each flipper. There are are 24–31 finely pointed teeth in each tooth row.

**Reproduction** Very little is known of this species' life history. Sexual maturity is reached at about

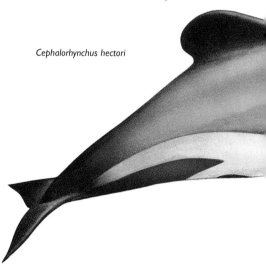

*Cephalorhynchus hectori*

4 feet (1.2 m) in males, and about 4½ feet (1.4 m) in females. Calving occurs during spring and early summer.

**Comment** Hector's dolphins can be attracted to boats, especially slow-moving boats, although they seldom bow ride. Dolphin watchers sometimes find that they will swim alongside a boat for a time, often following in its wake. In the past, these animals were caught for bait and currently they are often trapped accidentally in gill nets. Some parts of their habitat near the Banks Peninsula have been protected, but they are still endangered.

## KEY FACTS

♀ 5½ ft (1.7 m)

♂ 5 ft (1.5 m)

**Other names** None
**Size at birth** 23–27 in (60–70 cm)
**Weight** 110–132 lb (50–60 kg)
**Diet** A variety of small fish, from both the surface and sea floor
**Group size** Mainly small groups of 2–8 animals; occasionally larger pods
**Habitat** Shallow water, usually less than 984 ft (300 m) deep; near the shoreline
**Distribution** Found only in New Zealand waters, with greatest concentrations around the South Island

## DALL'S PORPOISE

The hyperactive Dall's porpoise acts more like an excited dolphin than a shy, retiring porpoise. Resident in the cold temperate North Pacific, Dall's porpoises will race around whale-watching boats, even riding the bow. Traveling just beneath the surface, at estimated speed of up to 35 miles (56 km) per hour, they push up a distinctive spray that looks like a "rooster tail." They do not leap out of the water, but nevertheless they can create hours of excitement for whale watchers.

**Appearance** This striking black-and-white-patterned porpoise, similar in color to the spectacled porpoise, has a wide girth and a triangular, two-tone dorsal fin. In contrast to its extremely stocky body, which belies the great speed it can attain, the head and beak are small, as are the pectoral fins and flukes. Most of the body is a rich black. A large patch of white occurs on the flank and ventral area, and there is a smaller patch on the trailing edge of the dorsal fin. The teeth are extremely small and spadelike; there are 19–29 on each side of the upper and lower jaws.

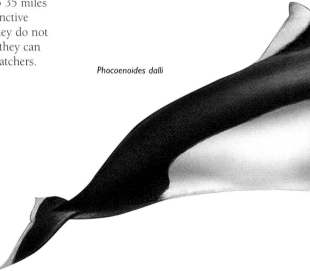

*Phocoenoides dalli*

**Reproduction** Males reach sexual maturity when they are about 6 feet (1.8 m) long. Females can breed when they are 5½ feet (1.7 m) long. Young are generally born in summer, after a gestation period of approximately 11.5 months.

**Comment** The Dall's porpoise is two to three times the bulk of other porpoise species. It takes its name from William H. Dall, the American zoologist who first noted them, describing them as large "porpoise-like" animals. He made his sightings off the coast of Alaska in the 1870s.

### KEY FACTS

♂ 7¼ ft (2.2 m)

♀ 7 ft (2.1 m)

**Other names** None
**Size at birth**
37–40 in (95–100 cm)
**Weight** 440 lb (200 kg)
**Diet** Midwater prey, such as squid; in coastal areas schooling fish
**Group size** 2–12; larger groups form for activities such as feeding
**Habitat** Cold waters off the continental shelf and slope
**Distribution** North Pacific and adjacent waters between about 30°N and 62°N

191

# SPECTACLED PORPOISE

Although porpoises are typically larger than dolphins, the spectacled porpoise is larger than both the tucuxi and Hector's dolphin. It is the least known of all the porpoises. Its patchy distribution in the cool waters of the Southern Hemisphere makes it difficult to study and there have been few sightings at sea. Only one or two at a time have ever been sighted.

**Appearance** The largest of the six species of porpoises, the spectacled porpoise has the stocky body shape and blunt snout that are characteristic of porpoises. The dorsal fin is large and rounded in males and triangular in females and the flukes are small. The pectoral fins are small and brilliant white in color. Like Dall's porpoise, the spectacled porpoise has distinctive black-and-white markings, and the pattern is strongly demarcated, with black dorsal and white ventral surfaces. The black patch around the eye surrounded by a fine white line gives this porpoise its common name. There is no trace of a beak, but there are distinctive black "lips." The teeth are spadelike; the upper jaw contains 17–23 pairs, and the lower jaw 16–20.

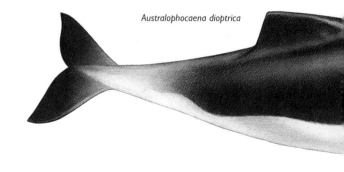

*Australophocaena dioptrica*

**Reproduction** As this species is rarely sighted, there is almost no life history information available on it. Some length measurements of pregnant females have been taken and these were about 6 feet (1.8 m) on average.

**Comment** Occasional strandings suggest that the spectacled porpoise may live in coastal waters, but a pattern of strandings and sightings at subantarctic islands points more strongly to a circumpolar distribution. Almost nothing is known of its diet, biology and behavior.

## KEY FACTS

♂ 7¼ ft (2.2 m)

♀ 6½ ft (2 m)

**Other names** Bicolor porpoise tonina (in Chilean waters)
**Size at birth** Probably 3 ft (1 m)
**Weight** Unknown as no adults have been weighed
**Diet** Unknown
**Group size** A difficult species to identify at sea unless closely observed; has been seen alone or in pairs
**Habitat** Sightings have occurred in rivers and channels as well as offshore waters
**Distribution** Probably circumpolar in subantarctic latitudes

193

# HARBOR PORPOISE

The harbor porpoise is the most commonly seen and studied member of its family, even though it is generally wary of boats and little of its body shows when it surfaces. Once glimpsed, it can be recognized by its low dorsal fin and absence of a beak. The blow of the harbor porpoise is rarely seen, but can be heard. Whale watchers unimpressed at first with the idea of seeing porpoises, come to enjoy the familiar "pop" that this porpoise makes when it spouts.

**Appearance** The harbor porpoise is a relatively small porpoise. It has the typical porpoise shape: a rounded head without a prominent forehead and almost no beak. The dorsal fin is low and triangular, and has a series of small, blunt spines on its leading edge, which are the main features used to identify this species. The pectoral fins are small and rounded, and the flukes are small. The overall dorsal color is a dark brown or dark gray, which fades to a whitish color on the belly. A thin, gray stripe extends on each side from the pectoral fin to the area near the gape of the mouth. There are 21–25 pairs of spadelike teeth in the lower jaw and 22–28 in the upper jaw.

*Phocoena phocoena*

**Reproduction** Both males and females are sexually mature when about 5 feet (1.5 m) long. The young are born during the summer after a gestation period of 11 months. Females generally have a calf every year, with no "rest" period in between. Calves are nursed for less than a year.

**Comment** The harbor porpoise is the shortest lived cetacean, rarely living beyond the age of 12 years. Even this short life is threatened by humans, who still hunt it in some places. It also gets caught in fishing nets and has suffered habitat loss near urban areas and shipping lanes.

**KEY FACTS**

♂♀ 6½ ft (2 m)

**Other names** Common porpoise, porpoise (English); *marsopa* (Spanish); *pourcil* (French)
**Size at birth** 27–35 in (70–90 cm)
**Weight** 88–132 lb (40–60 kg)
**Diet** Small schooling fish, such as herring or anchovy
**Group size** Usually fewer than 8; can be larger when feeding or migrating
**Habitat** Bays and estuaries containing murky waters caused by tidal races or coastal upwellings
**Distribution** Northern Hemisphere waters in temperate and subarctic areas

# AMAZON RIVER DOLPHIN

The largest and most commonly seen river
dolphin, the Amazon river dolphin is the only one
of the five river dolphin species to support regular
commercial tours. The only other dolphin to share
its habitat in the Amazon and Orinoco regions is
the tucuxi, which looks like a small bottlenose
dolphin and is smaller and more plainly colored
than the pinkish Amazon river dolphin. Amazon
river dolphins are said to be most active in the
early morning and late afternoon, and if so, they
follow the pattern of many tropical rain forest
creatures. They are usually seen alone or in pairs.

**Appearance**  Mainly pink, the
Amazon River dolphin has a long
beak with more than 100 teeth,
and a steep, bulbous forehead, or
melon. Instead of a true dorsal fin,
it has a wide-based dorsal ridge or
hump about two-thirds the way
down the body. The broad,
paddle-shaped pectoral fins are
relatively large and the flukes are
broad and pointed, with frayed
rear margins. This species is
unique in having differentiated
teeth. The front ones are conical,
like those of most dolphins; the
rear teeth are more like molars,
with an inside flange. This
suggests that they chew their food,
rather than swallowing it whole,
as other dolphins do.

*Inia geoffrensis*

♂ 8½ ft (2.6 m)

♀ 6½ ft (2 m)

**Other names** Boto (sometimes spelled bouto); *tonina* (Spanish)
**Size at birth** 31½ in (80 cm)
**Weight** ♂ 350 lb (160 kg),
♀ 220 lb (100 kg)
**Diet** A variety of fish, both bottom-dwelling and schooling; crustaceans
**Group size** Essentially solitary; fluctuating river depths can force animals into groups
**Habitat** Turbid river waters; forests and grasslands during floods
**Distribution** Drainage basins of the Amazon and Orinoco rivers in tropical South America

**Reproduction** Males reach sexual maturity when they are about 6½ feet (2 m) long; females when they are about 6 feet (1.8 m). Gestation period is thought to be between 10 and 11 months, with births occurring between May and July, during peak water levels. It is not unusual for females to be pregnant and lactating at the same time.

**Comment** This dolphin has the widest distribution and largest population of all the river dolphins. It is less affected by human population pressures than the three river dolphins of Asia, though the destruction of the tropical rain forest has caused a significant decline in its numbers. As a result, its long-term future is far from secure.

# Baiji

Barely 80 years after it was first described in scientific literature, the baiji is on the brink of extinction. Despite years of international conservation efforts, and despite its being declared a National Treasure of China, and being protected since 1975, it remains the most endangered of all cetaceans. According to some estimates there may be as few as 50 remaining individuals.

**Appearance** The baiji is predominantly a dark bluish gray color. Its long, narrow beak is slightly upturned, and it has a steep, rounded forehead. The dorsal fin is low and triangular, and the flippers are broad and rounded. The dark color on its back gradually fades down the sides toward the belly, lower jaw and the dorsal surface of the flippers and flukes, where it becomes a light gray or white. There are also some white markings on the face and sides of the tail stock. Each tooth row contains 31–38 conical teeth.

**Reproduction** Because this species is so rare—it is considered one of the rarest cetaceans, with a population numbering only in the hundreds—there is little biological

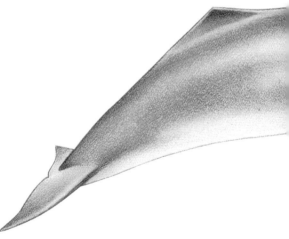

information available on it.
It is thought that calves are born between February and April.

**Comment** This species is most active from early evening to early morning and so is not often seen by humans. In any case, these animals are quiet, reserved and difficult to approach. In calm conditions, the blow may be heard as a high-pitched sneeze, although this quick spouting sound is difficult to distinguish from that of the finless porpoise, which is the only other cetacean species in its range, and which is much more numerous, more visible and easier to approach.

## KEY FACTS

♀ 8½ ft (2.6 m)

♂ 7½ ft (2.3 m)

**Other names** Yangtze river dolphin, Chinese river dolphin
**Size at birth** About 37 in (95 cm)
**Weight** ♂ 265 lb (125 kg), ♀ 350 lb (160 kg)
**Diet** Various fish species
**Group size** Generally in groups of 6 or fewer; individuals and pairs sometimes seen
**Habitat** Slow-moving river areas with established sandbars
**Distribution** Middle and lower reaches of the Yangtze River, China

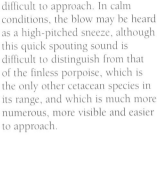

*Lipotes vexillifer*

199

# FRANCISCANA

Although closely related to the baiji, the only other member of the family Pontoporiidae, and to the other river dolphins, the franciscana lives only in the sea, in the temperate coastal waters of eastern South America. It feeds near the seabed and normally occurs alone or in small groups of up to five individuals. Until recently there were few records of live animals in the wild, but there have been many more sightings in recent years and several populations are now being studied.

**Appearance** Despite its exclusively marine habitat, the franciscana is usually classified as one of the river dolphins. Females are larger than males, but are otherwise similar. Both have a long, narrow beak that grows with age, a triangular dorsal fin, rounded at the tip, and prominent spatulate pectoral fins. The overall color is gray, darker on the back than on the ventral surface. There

are probably more than 200 teeth, with 51–58 in each row. Research suggests that different forms occur in different parts of its range, the northern form being smaller than the southern.

**Reproduction** Females weigh about 77 pounds (35 kg) at sexual maturity; males weigh slightly less at 64 pounds (29 kg). The

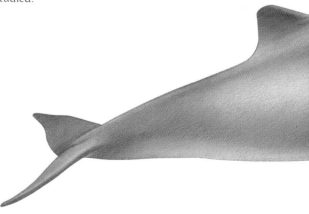

gestation period lasts for about 11 months and births occur in November and December.

**Comment** The five species of river dolphins are considered to be the most primitive groups of cetaceans, and the franciscana is regarded as the most primitive of this group. Although it lives only in the sea, it shows the same specialized riverine habitat adaptations of the other river dolphins: broad pectoral fins for maneuverability; and a mobile neck that allows the head to move from side to side, possibly for scanning with echolocation.

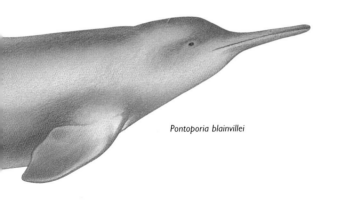

*Pontoporia blainvillei*

**KEY FACTS**

♀ 5¾ ft (1.75 m)

♂ 5 ft (1.5 m)

**Other names** La Plata dolphin
**Size at birth** About 30 in (75 cm)
**Weight** ♀ 117 lb (53 kg),
♂ 95 lb (43 kg)
**Diet** Largely bottom-dwelling prey such as shrimp, squid, octopus, fish and crustaceans
**Group size** Probably does not form large groups
**Habitat** Primarily a marine species in shallow inshore waters
**Distribution** Coastal waters of eastern South America, from Peninsula Valdes in Argentina to the Doce River in Brazil

## GANGES RIVER DOLPHIN

The Ganges river dolphin is believed to be closely related to the now extinct, but once widespread, shark-toothed dolphins—members of the family Squalodontidae. This endangered species moves and feeds in a murky riverine environment using echolocation. Its eyes, which are capable only of distinguishing light from dark, are tiny and effectively nonfunctional.

**Appearance** The exceptionally long and slender beak of this species contains 26–39 thin, backward-curving teeth on each side of the upper jaw and 26–35 on each side of the lower jaw. The anterior teeth are longer than the rear ones, and these extend outside the closed mouth like a pair of forceps. This feature, combined with the small, rounded melon set off from the fat, chunky body, contributes to the strange appearance of this relatively small dolphin. Its body color is predominantly gray-brown, and there are sometimes some pinkish areas on the belly. There is no true dorsal fin, but there is a low triangular hump on the back. The distinctive pectoral fins are broad and paddle-shaped and the flukes are pointed and swept back. The very tiny eyes, set in a fold of skin just above the corner of the mouth, are barely visible.

**Reproduction** Little life history information is available on this species. The estimated gestation period is about eight to nine months. Young can be born any time, although there are probably peaks in December–January and March–May.

**Comment** This dolphin is almost identical to its closest living relative, the Indus river dolphin, *Platanista minor*. Only some differences in the structure of the skull have caused them to be considered separate species.

**KEY FACTS**

♀ 8¼ ft (2.5 m)

♂ 7 ft (2.1 m)

**Other names** Susu or Ganges susu; blind river dolphin; gangetic dolphin
**Size at birth**
25½–35½ ins (65–90 cm)
**Weight** 185 lb (85 kg)
**Diet** A variety of vertebrate and invertebrate prey, such as fish, crustaceans and mollusks
**Group size** Small groups are the norm; also seen in pairs and alone
**Habitat** Slow-moving river waters; some areas in fast-moving, clear rivers
**Distribution** India, Bangladesh, parts of Nepal and Bhutan river systems

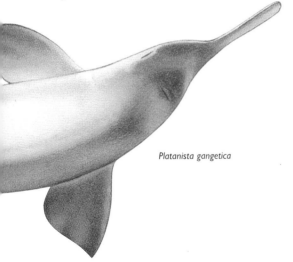

*Platanista gangetica*

203

# PART THREE

# WHALES AND PEOPLE

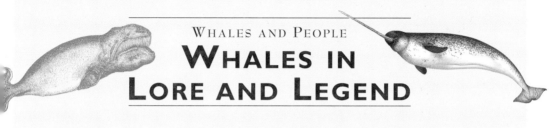

# WHALES IN LORE AND LEGEND

Archeological evidence shows that humans have long been fascinated by whales and dolphins. Five thousand years before the classical Mediterranean civilizations celebrated dolphins in art and poetry, neolithic societies in Norway etched whales in rock. Other vanished hunting peoples, such as the Dorset culture of northern Canada, carved graceful representations of whales and seals in ivory and rock. Ancient societies that still survive today, such as the Inuit of Alaska and the Nootka of British Columbia, also have fine traditions of artwork, dance and myths that feature cetaceans. Inuit hunters went to great lengths to please the spirits of whales and other animals they depended on.

# LORE AND LEGEND

**The icon of the dolphin abounds in classical Greek mythology. Indeed, the word "dolphin" derives from *delphys*, Greek for womb, and in one version of Greek mythology, all creation emerged from the womb of a dolphin.**

**Archetypal images** Other archetypal images include that of a youth riding a dolphin. The Roman writer Pliny the Elder (23–79 B.C.) tells the story of a boy who rode on the back of a friendly dolphin called Simo. In Greece there was a similar story of the dolphin of Iassos, who fell in love with a beautiful boy and allowed him to ride on its back, even taking him far out to sea. In both of these stories, the boy dies, and the dolphin then dies of grief. In a similar vein is the myth of the sailor who is saved by dolphins.

**Fearsome whales** Unlike the ancient Greeks, other cultures depicted whales as terrifying, tusked, scaled monsters. Because of their size and power, whales in many old stories, such as the biblical tale of Jonah and the

### JONAH

Far left and left: The best known whale story in the Bible is about Jonah. While he was sailing to the city of Nineveh, a great storm erupted, and the ship's crew threw Jonah overboard. A whale swallowed Jonah, who spent three days and three nights in the whale's belly. Finally, the whale spat Jonah out on to land, and he proceeded safely on his journey to Nineveh.

### Friends and foes

In the North Atlantic, whales were prominent in myths as well as true accounts. Red-headed whales were feared by Icelandic seamen. They believed they were born of a curse, and specialized in destroying ships and eating their crews. Other whales, such as fin whales, were regarded as friendly creatures, and many people believed that they helped humans by driving herring inshore. Norwegian fishermen were angered when modern technology enabled these whales to be killed.

### MONSTER OF THE DEEP

This nineteenth-century etching of a sperm whale about to destroy a ship reflects the myth of the essentially destructive nature of large whales.

whale, are often fearsome animals. In a similar nineteenth-century tale, a swallowed whaleman was bleached white by the whale's gastric juices. There is a story that during Alexander the Great's campaign in India in 4 B.C., his men became so alarmed by the mass blowing of whales around them that they dropped their oars in terror.

# LORE AND LEGEND continued

*Narwhal*

**Lore or no lore**  Every culture familiar with whales has some lore about them. Myths and tales about whales come from such diverse places as India, Africa, Korea and Polynesia. Interestingly, a lack of folk tales about whales in Hawaii has led researchers to conclude that the humpback whale now migrating there may have done so only during the past 200 years.

**Whalers' lore**  In Europe, as commercial whaling took hold in the sixteenth century, the mythology of whales as fantastic creatures began to disappear. It was replaced by a more pragmatic view of whales as commercial products. However, there was still a great appreciation of them by those who actually sought them on the oceans. Aspects of this era can still be glimpsed in the whalers' songs and shanties, many of which have been preserved, and in scrimshaw, the delicate carving made on whale teeth.

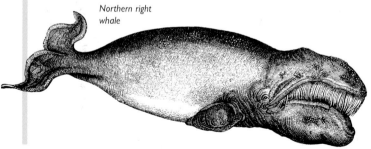

*Northern right whale*

## UNICORNS AND MONSTERS

Above: It is quite possible that the tusk of the male narwhal was the original inspiration for the myth of the unicorn. It is certainly true that in medieval Europe narwhal tusks were highly prized.

Left: Grotesque representations of whales in some nineteenth-century etchings, such as this one of a northern right whale, helped foster the myth of whales as fearsome monsters.

## Whales in fiction

The life and adventure of whaling have been the subjects of numerous books. Many of them have been factual accounts of nineteenth-century whaling by whalers such as Frank Bullen and William Scoresby. In fiction, the best known of all whaling stories is undoubtedly *Moby Dick, or The White Whale* by Herman Melville. Melville spent several years as a whaler, and his novel is full of accurate observations. The image of the "whale island" was echoed in another literary classic, Jules Verne's *Twenty Thousand Leagues under the Sea*, in which Captain Nemo's submarine, the *Nautilus,* is mistaken for a gigantic whale.

### MOBY DICK

In this colorful illustration of a scene from Herman Melville's novel *Moby Dick*, Starbuck, one of the main characters in the book, urges his men on as they row through the waves in pursuit of a sperm whale.

### Modern myths

In more recent times, whales continued to feature in literature—in novels such as *The Deep Range*, by Arthur C. Clarke—as well as in songs, paintings and photography. For many people today, whales have taken on a spiritual significance, and are frequently associated with the wellbeing of the Earth.

# USING AND PROTECTING WHALES

Whales have probably been hunted since the beginning of human history. In earliest times, coastal communities would have taken advantage of dead whales washed ashore, using the meat as a source of food and other parts of the carcasses for a variety of different products. Our Stone Age ancestors used whalebones as rafters for their dwellings, while the Vikings made chairs from whale vertebrae. Whaling as an industry dates back almost 1,000 years, and over the centuries whales have been hunted commercially, in many cases almost to extinction. Only in the second half of the twentieth century did the emphasis begin to swing from exploitation to protection and preservation.

# THE WHALING INDUSTRY

For people of the earliest times, stranded whales provided great bounty. Whalemeat, blubber, sinews, bones and baleen all had valuable uses. For those observing whales that ventured into bays, the next step may have been to drive them ashore, using canoes or similar craft. Echoes of such drive fisheries can be seen today in Japan and the Faeroe Islands, near Iceland. The final step was the transition to killing whales offshore.

**FLENSING**
This illustration, published around 1813, illustrates the centuries-old technique of flensing, or cutting up, a whale that has been lashed to the whaleship. The picture, however, conveys nothing of the danger and discomfort of a whaler's working life.

**Simple craft** The simple technology required to drive whales ashore was employed by the Inuit and other northern peoples until very recently. Primitive dugout canoes were sometimes used, as by the Makah people of the northwest Pacific, who killed whales up to 20 miles (32 km) offshore. Indigenous whaling was also conducted by the Vikings and their descendants in the North Atlantic Ocean.

**Basque beginnings** Whaling as a commercial activity began with the Basques in the Bay of Biscay, northern Spain. By the twelfth century, bay whaling for right whales had achieved a degree of economic importance. The Basques were great seafarers and explorers, and by the sixteenth century, they had expanded their

### HEAVILY HUNTED
Northern bottlenose whales have been hunted more extensively than any other species of beaked whales.

activities as far afield as Newfoundland. The British then discovered right and bowhead whales in Norway, around Spitsbergen, and employed Basque whalers to hunt them.

**Dutch whalers** In the early 1600s, Holland emerged as a whaling power. The Dutch began the practice of killing whales at sea and cutting them up alongside their boats, pursuing them farther and farther north as bay-whaling fell off because of declining whale numbers. The whales were boiled down, and "tried out" on deck, a procedure that could result in a fire which damaged or destroyed the ship.

**Whaling spreads** Colonists in New England started whaling early in the eighteenth century, when whale oil became increasingly important for street lighting and for use in textile manufacture. By late in the century, England was *the* global maritime power, with the largest whaling fleet. The prime whaling sites were then in Davis Strait, between Canada and Greenland, though at this time Samuel Enderby started the Southern Hemisphere fishery, which expanded into the Pacific Ocean in 1789, opening up new, lucrative whaling grounds.

### DANGER
This nineteenth-century illustration depicts the perils involved in rowing out from the whaleship to pursue and harpoon whales.

215

# THE WHALING INDUSTRY continued

**HUNTED FOR OIL**
Sperm whales were hunted mainly for their oil. Sperm-whale oil burns brighter and with less odor than other whale oils, and spermaceti oil is one of the best lubricating oils known.

**Exploitation** The unchecked exploitation of right and bowhead whales took its toll, and by 1850 they were no longer commercially viable in the Atlantic and South Pacific. By now, attention had shifted largely to sperm whales. While French, British and Australian whalers were also at work, the New Englanders, known as the Yankee whalers, now dominated the world scene. They discovered and wiped out bowheads in the Bering Sea in the 1840s, severely reduced the numbers of gray whales off the United States Pacific coast, and killed huge numbers of sperm whales. Their downfall was the discovery of petroleum as a fuel in 1859, which soon rendered sperm oil valueless.

**Radical changes** In 1864, a development occurred that was to change the face of whaling. Few right whales remained, so Svend Foyn, a Norwegian sealer, pondered the abundance of rorquals. Except for the slow humpback, these whales could not be caught with rowed whaleboats. Foyn refined designs for a cannon-fired, barbed, explosive harpoon, mounted on the bow of a fast steam-powered ship, with a winch for retrieving the whale and a shock absorber to relieve the strains on the line. This became known as a catcher vessel. By 1886, 19 companies were using

## THE AFTERMATH OF WHALING

In just a few hundred years, countless millions of great whales were slaughtered. Two million whales were killed in the Southern Ocean alone. By the time whales were given official protection, it was almost too late, and some species may never recover. The rarest whale in the world—the northern right whale—came so close to extinction that even after more than 60 years of protection there are only about 300 survivors. The bowhead whale has all but disappeared from much of its former range. But, against all the odds, some whales appear to be re-establishing themselves. The gray whale is the ultimate success story. Although the North Atlantic stock is now extinct and only a remnant population exists in the western North Pacific, it has made a dramatic recovery in the eastern North Pacific, and is believed to be as abundant now as in the days before whaling. The figures to the right are very approximate minimum population estimates.

| Species | Original | Present |
| --- | --- | --- |
| Sperm whale | 2,500,000 | 1,500,000 |
| Blue whale | 300,000 | 6,000 |
| Fin whale | 600,000 | 60,000 |
| Sei whale | 250,000 | 40,000 |
| Bryde's whale | 90,000 | 90,000 |
| Minke whale | 850,000 | 936,000 |
| Humpback whale | 250,000 | 25,000 |
| Gray whale | 20,000 | 26,000 |
| Northern right whale | 200,000 | 300 |
| Southern right whale | 150,000 | 7,000 |
| Bowhead whale | 30,000 | 7,500 |

### BLUE WHALES

Blue whales were one of the three species of rorquals most frequently caught by Norwegian whalers in the late nineteenth century. Fin and sei whales were the other two.

this new technology in Norway. In 1895, a Norwegian station opened in Japan. "Norwegian whaling" was set to become the model for the new century.

**Declining rorquals** After factory ships appeared, the whales were towed in by catchers to be flensed in the water alongside, then rendered to oil. By the start of World War I, rorquals were in decline in the North Atlantic. Large numbers of rorquals were known to exist in Antarctic waters, but the distance from European ports delayed serious attempts to commence whaling there.

Using and Protecting Whales

**STILL VULNERABLE**
Whaling operations have drastically reduced the numbers of humpback whales, one of the best known and most popular species with whale watchers. While numbers are now probably on the increase, these whales are still considered vulnerable.

**Antarctic slaughter**  The greatest whale slaughter of them all began in November 1904, after Argentinian business interests agreed to back Norwegian Carl Anton Larsen in a whaling venture at South Georgia Island. Early seasons there brought big catches of humpbacks. By 1911, there were seven shore stations on South Georgia and other stations on other islands near the Antarctic Peninsula. Antarctic whaling expanded quickly in the 1920s and 1930s. In the 1930–31 season alone, 41 factory ships killed more than 37,000 whales.

**Attempts at control**  World War II brought some respite from the pressure of whaling, but after the war, even more nations than before entered the fray. In 1947, the International Convention for the Regulation of Whaling, administered by the International Whaling Commission (IWC), came into being, but, as it had no powers of enforcement, whale numbers continued to decline. However, growing pressure from conservationists finally achieved some results. By the mid-1960s, all nations, except Japan and the USSR, had withdrawn from Antarctic whaling, and in 1986, a "moratorium" on commercial whaling worldwide was adopted by the IWC. The Soviets withdrew from the Antarctic in 1987, leaving only the Japanese operating in the region. Today, so-called "small-type coastal whaling" still occurs in Japan, Norway and Greenland, as well as in some other places. As well, subsistence whaling has survived in some areas, such as Alaska and the Philippines.

## KEY TECHNOLOGICAL DEVELOPMENTS IN MODERN WHALING

Until just over a century ago, the technique of whaling had barely changed for more than 700 years. But in the 1850s, the era of modern commercial whaling began with a vengeance—and the whalers have not looked back since.

**1852** The first successful explosive harpoon was invented. Known as the bomb-lance, it consisted of an explosive missile armed with a time-delay fuse that killed or mortally wounded the whales.

**1857** The first auxiliary steam engines were installed in British whaling ships and, in the years that followed, many other whalers installed similar engines in their vessels.

**1859** The first purpose-built steam whaling ships were launched. The extra power increased their speed and safety, though in the whaling grounds, whalers continued to hunt from rowing boats.

**1863** Norwegian Svend Foyn built a new steam-driven schooner called *Spes et Fides* (meaning "Hope and Faith").

The first of the modern whale catchers, this combined the functions of the open rowing boat and the ship in a single vessel. It was relatively easy to maneuver and yet fast enough to chase the whales by itself. No species of whale was now safe.

**1865** A whaling captain from New Bedford, in the United States, invented the darting gun, a kind of explosive harpoon with the accuracy of a conventional harpoon.

**1868** After several seasons of experimentation, Svend Foyn developed an explosive harpoon that could be fired from a cannon mounted on a swivel in the bow of a whaling vessel.

*Northern right whale*

The cannon was solidly made to absorb the recoil and so well balanced that it could be aimed with great accuracy.

Screwed to the tip of the harpoon was a grenade, consisting of a detonator and a sack of black gunpowder in a steel container equipped with barbs. The barbs were designed to open on impact, ensuring that the harpoon was firmly embedded in the animal's flesh, and the grenade exploded inside its body two or thee seconds later. This awful weapon precipitated an enormous increase in whaling activity worldwide and is still in use today, albeit in modified form.

**1925** The growth of the whaling industry was limited by a need to return constantly to shore-based stations in order to process the whales. The final dramatic development—floating factory ships—solved this problem.

The new ships were designed to accompany fleets of catcher boats far out to sea and, with stern slipways to winch the whales on board, gave a new level of efficiency to the hunt. It was in 1925 that the first factory ship arrived on the Antarctic whaling grounds.

# WHALE PRODUCTS

Until recently, whales provided products that were regarded as necessities in industrialized societies. Now the situation has changed, and advances in technology mean that, with the exception of whale meat, most of the products of whaling can be synthesized from other sources.

**Whale oil** Oil was the main commercial product throughout the era of commercial whaling. It lubricated the machinery of the Industrial Revolution, and fired the street lamps of London and New York. Electricity ended its use for lighting, but new processes made it usable in the production of soap, margarine and cooking fats. More recent uses of whale oil include waxes, paints, varnishes, preservatives and pharmaceuticals—in fact, almost any product that needs

**SCRIMSHAW AND ARCHES**
Above: This decorative entrance arch is typical of many that were made out of the jawbones of baleen whales. Left: Sperm whale teeth carved by whalers in their spare time are now highly valued as collectable folk art. They are known as scrimshaw.

oil as part of its ingredients. Spermaceti oil, a fine lubricating oil, has been used, among other things, for missile inertial guidance. However, whale oils have now been replaced by vegetable oils.

**Baleen and bones** Baleen, or "whalebone," was a valuable product with many uses. Its flexibility and stiffness made it useful in watch springs, umbrella ribs, brassieres, brushes and corsets, among many other things.

## AMBERGRIS: WHALE GOLD

Ambergris was once regarded as the most valuable of whale products. It could be obtained without encountering the whale itself. Ambergris occurs as a waxy, solidified lump occasionally found floating in the sea, or washed ashore. It is formed in the lower intestines of some sperm whales, and disgorged when the whales vomit. Despite its unpleasant origin, "a little whiff of it," according to the British poet Alexander Pope, "...is very agreeable." Primarily made of ambrein, a fatty substance similar to cholesterol, it hardens on exposure to air, and often contains squid beaks. Whenever whalers found a lump of ambergris in the sea, or removed it from a recently killed sperm whale, they whooped and cheered. It was worth its weight in gold. Originally used as a medicine to treat indigestion, convulsions and a variety of other ailments, and also as an aphrodisiac, it became invaluable later as a fixative in perfumes and for making cosmetics. Since the early 1900s, some huge lumps of ambergris have been found, a few of them looking more like giant rocks or boulders than something that could have come out of a sperm whale. The largest ever recorded, weighing an incredible 1,400 pounds (635 kg), was found near New Zealand by a British whaler.

**HIT HARD**
During periods of heavy whaling, the largest whales were prime targets: Female baleen whales and male sperm whales (left), the largest toothed whales, were the hardest hit.

Teeth were used for buttons and piano keys, as well as for the decorative scrimshaw for which they are best known. During the industrial whaling era, whale bones were ground into fertilizer, but in earlier days they were used as building materials, and the paired jawbones of baleen whales were often used as entrance arches.

221

# WHALES IN DANGER

Since the beginning of the Industrial Revolution, more than 200 years ago, humans have greatly modified the natural environment. Environmental degradation, especially in recent decades, has created a succession of crises that have had a serious impact on cetaceans.

**Habitat degradation** Inshore habitats of cetaceans have been affected by such factors as the damming of rivers, the draining and filling of mangrove swamps, the development of coastal foreshores and the discharges of industrial waste and sewage. Industrial development has also brought serious pollution to areas of open ocean. Items of litter, such as fragments of fishing net that can entangle whales and plastic bags that they mistake for squid and eat, are also potential hazards.

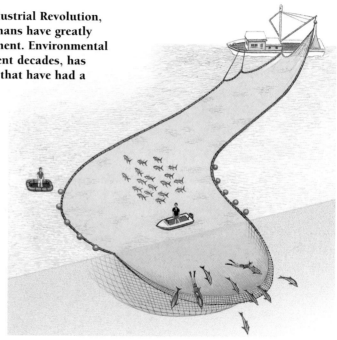

**Chemicals** Heavy metals, such as mercury, which concentrate in whales' brains and other organs, pose an insidious threat, as do organochlorines such as DDT and PCBs. Carried by ocean currents, these chemicals become more concentrated as they move up through the food chain.

**Climate change** Climate change arising from human activity may yet prove to be the most critical threat to whales' survival. Rising sea temperatures would modify patterns of currents and upwelling and could cause polar seas to contract, thus reducing suitable habitats for whale prey.

**NETTING**

Purse-seine netting is used to catch tuna, but has also caused the deaths of many dolphins, which become trapped in the net. Divers sometimes save dolphins by helping them out over the edge before the net is drawn shut.

## The Rarest Cetaceans

| Species and Distribution | Population | Notes |
| --- | --- | --- |
| **Yangtze river dolphin or baiji** | | |
| Yangtze River, China (middle and lower reaches) | Fewer than 100 (possibly fewer than 50) | Now very little chance of rescuing this species. It is likely to become the first cetacean to become extinct in historical times. |
| **Vaquita or Gulf of California porpoise** | | |
| Extreme northern end of the Gulf of California (Sea of Cortez), Mexico | Fewer than 200 | Has the most restricted distribution of any marine cetacean; most commonly seen around the Colorado River delta. |
| **Northern right whale** | | |
| Western North Atlantic (occasional records from eastern North Atlantic and eastern North Pacific) | Fewer than 320 | Officially protected for more than 60 years, it has never recovered from being hunted almost to extinction by commercial whalers. |
| **Indus river dolphin or bhulan** | | |
| Indus River, Pakistan (mainly along 100-mile [160-km] stretch between Sukkur and Guddu barrages) | Fewer than 500 | Since the 1930s, barrages have split the dwindling population into isolated pockets. |
| **Heaviside's dolphin** | | |
| Coastal waters of western South Africa and Namibia | Fewer than 1,000 | The world's rarest marine dolphin, with a very restricted distribution. |

# WHALE CONSERVATION

In recent years, much publicity has been given to the plight of cetaceans and threats to their survival. As people have become aware of the issues involved, and familiar with the findings of researchers, governments have come under greater pressure to promote whale conservation.

**Slow to respond** Despite the pressure, governments are often slow to respond, even to widespread public opinion. It has taken many years, for example, for warnings about global warming to be heeded at official levels.

**Organizations** Much of the initiative for change comes from animal welfare and conservation organizations, which act as pressure groups and actively publicize environmental issues. In the United States, these groups

### SUCCESS STORY

The gray whale is, perhaps, the ultimate whale conservation success story. Although its range has been severely curtailed as a result of whaling, this species has made a dramatic recovery in the eastern North Pacific. It is believed to be as abundant now as in the days before whaling.

## WORLDWIDE PROTECTION

The first whale to be given worldwide protection from commercial whaling was the bowhead, in the early 1930s. Most other species have been afforded regional or worldwide protection in the years since. This culminated, in 1986, with a moratorium on commercial whaling which, finally, granted worldwide protection for all the great whales. Unfortunately, the killing often continued long after official protection was declared (and, in some cases, continues still today) but the following dates still have considerable significance:

1931  Bowhead whale (became U.S. law in 1935)
1935  Northern right whale and southern right whale
1946  Gray whale
1966  Humpback whale and blue whale
1979  Sei whale (except in the Denmark Strait west of Iceland)
1984  Sperm whale
1986  IWC moratorium takes effect

*gray whale*

range from the Humane Society, a relatively conservative group, to the radical Sea Shepherd Society. There are numerous other groups at different points on this spectrum. The largest organization in the world that is dedicated to the conservation, welfare and appreciation of cetaceans is the British-based Whale and Dolphin Conservation Society. All these organizations rely heavily on public support, for both their finances and the personnel needed to undertake their campaigns.

**Public involvement** Thanks largely to public concern, expressed in demonstrations and other forms of representation, former whaling nations, such as Australia and the United States, have a political mandate to promote whale conservation at the International Whaling Commission (IWC). Whaling, however, is an issue that easily involves human sympathies and has relatively clear-cut solutions. People are less aware of the other problems facing whales and of the ways in which these problems are a consequence of our modern lifestyle. For example, each of us contributes to global warming through our energy use; we use products made from the toxic chemicals that pollute the oceans; and many of us eat driftnet-caught tuna. Only by becoming actively involved by, for example, reducing our energy consumption, buying only environmentally safe products and opposing detrimental coastal developments, can we make a positive contribution to solving whale conservation and other environmental problems.

# WHALE CONSERVATION continued

**The IWC** Ever since 1946, government representatives from around the world have met every year, under the auspices of the IWC, to discuss whaling. The IWC was established originally to make possible the orderly development of the whaling industry. It actively encouraged whaling and, as a result, more than two million whales were killed during the organization's first 30 years. More recently, the IWC has been working toward better protection of cetaceans. But some of its

**Commercial and Scientific Whale Catches under the IWC**

| Country | Region | Species | 1994 | 1995 | 1996 |
|---------|--------|---------|------|------|------|
| Norway | Northeast Atlantic | Minke whale | 279 | 217 | 388 |
| Japan | North Pacific | Minke whale | 21 | 100 | 77 |
| Japan | Antarctica | Minke whale | 330 | 440 | 440 |
| Total | | | 630 | 757 | 905 |

**IWC LOGO**
Although it is frequently criticized, the IWC has long been the world's only means of supervising whalers, whose declining profits led them to pursue whale species indiscriminately.

39 member countries are still pro-whaling. Consequently, IWC debates are frequently heated and can involve bribery and threats.

**A breakthrough**
In 1982, there was a major breakthrough when IWC members voted for an indefinite moratorium on commercial whaling. But this world peace treaty for the whales left too many loopholes to work effectively. Since then, more than 57,000 whales have been killed. Even since 1986, when the whaling ban actually came into effect, Japan, Norway, Iceland, Korea, and indigenous whalers in several other countries, have killed more than 21,000 whales between them.

**Whale sanctuaries** Whale sanctuaries are zones where commercial whaling is prohibited, and the whales receive special protection. In 1979, the IWC, with the agreement of all nations bordering the Indian Ocean, declared this great body of water to be a whale sanctuary. In 1991, the Republic of Ireland became the first nation to act independently by declaring its waters to be a whale sanctuary. In May 1994, members of the IWC approved the declaration of the huge Southern Ocean Whale Sanctuary, which covers all Antarctic waters and offers at least nominal protection to the world's largest whale populations. Japan strongly opposed the declaration of this sanctuary, maintaining that culling of minke whales in commercial quantities does not threaten their survival. Other small sanctuaries, which have recently been established in Hawaii, Australia and New Zealand, provide further evidence of the effectiveness of concerted public pressure.

**The future** At the 1996 IWC meeting, several countries stated their opposition to whaling under any circumstances, a controversial position which, however, reflected a moral view shared by millions of people worldwide. As we have seen, despite this declaration, a number of countries still continue to hunt and kill whales in large numbers. At least the IWC provides a forum in which the

**SURVIVING AGAINST ODDS**
Minke whales are the only baleen whales still being regularly hunted by commercial whalers. Despite this, some estimates put their present numbers at almost a million individuals.

problems of whaling are kept firmly to the fore. How the IWC will evolve in future, only time will tell. What is certain is that the whales are not saved yet.

227

# INTERACTING WITH WHALES

There are many known incidents in which whales have initiated "friendly" contact with humans. Given our past treatment of them, why are they not afraid of us? Perhaps they are curious about alien creatures in their environment, or perhaps they simply enjoy the company.

**Ancient times** Numerous stories suggest that there has always been an affinity between humans and dolphins. As far back as A.D. 66, the Greek writer Plutarch wrote that dolphins had a gift for "unselfish friendship."

**Jack and Opo** One of the first documented examples of cetacean friendliness in modern times is that of a Risso's dolphin known as Pelorus Jack. For 24 years—until 1912—he escorted steamers past the mouth of Pelorus Sound in Cook Strait, New Zealand. In

**MONKEY MIA**
At Monkey Mia, in Western Australia, bottlenose dolphins come fearlessly up to the many tourists who frequent the area, accepting pieces of fish from the visitors' hands and allowing themselves to be petted and stroked.

### HARMLESS TO HUMANS
Because orcas are voracious predators, they are often called killer whales. However, there is no recorded case of an orca in the wild ever killing a human being. In fact orcas often show a friendly interest in people in boats.

1955, a female bottlenose dolphin, which was given the name Opo, began approaching people on the beach in Hokianga Harbour in the far northeast of New Zealand's North Island.

### Helping out
There are numerous accounts of various dolphins that aided mariners who were in difficulties, or warned sailors of unseeen hazards. The noted French yachtsman Bernard Moitessier told of how dolphins caused him to avoid running aground on Stewart Island, off the southern tip of New Zealand in 1968, by making passes past his boat and then turning right, thus guiding him to safety.

**Larger whales**  Larger whales also seem to seek and enjoy human contact. Minke whales are noted for their "ship-seeking" behavior, while others, including humpbacks, can appear fascinated by smaller craft and their human occupants, and may repeatedly circle and dive underneath the boat, or spyhop frequently. Whales are usually careful not to bump boats. They will often approach and interact with swimmers, even to the point of physical contact. Whales are quite gentle.

### FRIENDLY BOTTLENOSE
The bottlenose dolphins at Monkey Mia willingly "play up" to their admiring human audience.

229

# WHALES IN CAPTIVITY

The first time cetaceans were kept in captivity was in 1913, when harbor porpoises were put on display in a New York aquarium. Since then, many other toothed whales have been kept in captivity, including bottlenose dolphins, pilot whales, orcas, belugas and many others.

**Unfamiliar uses** Some captive cetaceans have been put to use for both commercial and military purposes. While most people are familiar with dolphinariums, where trained whales and dolphins entertain paying audiences, only a few would be familiar with the reputed uses of whales for, among other things, the recovery of missiles, the placement of mines, and even the carrying of weapons to attack and kill enemy divers.

### GOING THROUGH THEIR PACES

A group of human visitors watch a pair of trained dolphins going through their paces in a dolphinarium. Many animal welfare groups are strongly opposed to the use of dolphins for entertainment, and even to keeping them in captivity for purposes of research.

### A STUDY IN CONTRASTS
The heads of a short-finned pilot whale and a bottlenose dolphin (bottom) make an interesting study in contrasts in this dolphinarium setting.

dolphin in the wild. Exposure to captive animals, they claim, increases public awareness and understanding of cetaceans. They point to famous captives such as Namu, an orca that was kept in a Vancouver dolphinarium in the early 1960s. At a time when orcas were persecuted because they were perceived as dangerous killers, Namu's charm helped to create a sympathetic attitude towards this species.

**Research** The opportunity for research is a common argument in favor of captivity. In

**Arguments for captivity**
Opinion for and against the captivity of cetaceans is strongly polarized. Those in favor argue that it is vital for educational purposes, and that most people would never see a whale or a

the wild, cetaceans are often hard to locate, let alone observe. The study of many captive species has yielded valuable insights into important aspects of their life, including breeding and social behavior, sleep and dreaming patterns, and means of communication.

### PORPOISING
These trained captive dolphins are "porpoising" for the edification of their human audience.

**Public displays** Criticisms of public displays as mere circus acts have resulted in a trend to incorporate natural behavior into these exhibitions. And in answer to charges that many dolphins have been captured from the wild, there are figures showing that in the United States 40 percent of dolphins were, in fact, born in captivity. Dolphins in captivity form social groups, and they produce calves that know only captivity as a way of life. Dolphins may also play a role in human therapy, by eliciting responses from people suffering from autism and other socially debilitating conditions and diseases.

**Arguments against captivity** People who object to whales being kept in captivity claim that it is demeaning for the animals and

**WELL STUDIED**
Bottlenose dolphins are the cetacean species most likely to be kept in captivity. It is possible that animals born and bred in captivity develop different behavior patterns than animals in the wild.

point to the stress that confinement causes. They claim that pools, no matter how commodious, cannot begin to replicate the open ocean. A pool lacks the varied stimulation provided by the natural environment, while its concrete surface creates a confusing auditory world of echoes. There is also a constant risk of disease and infection from food or unclean water.

**Social structures** Opponents also point to artificial social structures, and consequent aberrant behaviors that develop in captivity. In the wild, groups are often fluid—an animal that deviates from a group's behavior patterns may join another group. But within the confines of a pool, it is impossible for them to change groups. Even normal sexual behavior may not be possible in captivity. For example, wild males of many species wander from group to group, seeking females to mate with. In a pool, they may mate only with females in the same group. It is impossible to predict what the long-term psychological and behavioral consequences of keeping whales in such constricting conditions will be. However, critics point to recent events, such as an instance of an orca killing its trainer, as an indication that all is far from well.

### CUDDLING UP

People love interacting with dolphins, and the chances to do so in the wild are severely limited. However, the practice of keeping captive animals for the amusement of humans is often condemned as demeaning and cruel.

### CAPTIVE ORCA

In captivity orcas, assured of a plentiful supply of food, will often peaceably share a pool with other species of whales and dolphins that they would prey upon in the wild. Orcas are the most popular cetaceans in large marine parks around the world, often attracting huge crowds.

### A special case

Most researchers would reject the argument that captivity is a form of conservation. The baiji may be an exception. Fewer than 50 baijis are thought to exist in the wild, where they face threats ranging from overfishing to dam construction.

Perhaps establishing a breeding colony in a semi-natural reserve may be the only way to save this species from what would otherwise be certain extinction.

233

# WHALE RESEARCH

Despite a flow of new information, we know surprisingly little about the majority of cetacean species and our knowledge of the others is very patchy. We have learned enough to start asking the right questions, yet the deeper we delve, the more we realize there is still much to learn.

**Difficulties**  The problem is that these are among the most difficult animals in the world to study. They often live in remote areas far out to sea, spending most of their lives underwater, and showing little when they rise to the surface to breathe.

**Dead animals**  In the early days of cetacean research, the little information we had came mainly from dead animals washed ashore or killed by whalers and fishers. Even today, professional post-mortems can teach us a great deal about poorly known species, such as beaked whales.

**Captive animals**  In the mid-1800s, another source of information became available. Since then, biologists have been able to study captive animals—usually dolphins and other small species that can be contained in a concrete tank—with varying results. However, at the very least, conclusions drawn from research

**DOLPHIN RESEARCH**
Much of the research and theorizing about the intelligence of cetaceans is based on information gathered from studies carried out on captive dolphins.

on captive animals must be treated with caution. Many studies can be carried out satisfactorily only under natural conditions. But there are advantages to studying cetaceans under controlled conditions. They can be observed at close range for 24 hours a day. Knowing such things as their age, sex, reproductive status and level of dominance is another major benefit. It is also useful to be able to undertake specific scientific experiments, under tightly controlled conditions, on everything from sleep needs to the physiology of diving.

**Going out to sea** A great deal of information can be obtained only by studying the animals, wild and free, in their natural environment. Few people took up this enormous challenge until the 1960s and early 1970s, and it is only in the past decade or so that research into wild cetaceans really developed into the sophisticated and popular branch of science we know today. Early pioneers focused mainly on counting whales at sea. Observers were posted at lookouts on land, in boats, or in light aircraft, and used relatively simple methods to calculate population and group sizes. These days many more factors are taken into account in making these calculations. As well, research has progressed to areas such as social and behavioral studies, supported by very careful and detailed note-taking.

### EAVESDROPPING ON SPERM WHALES

In 1983, Dr. Hal Whitehead and several companions sailed into the Indian Ocean in the tiny 33-foot (10 m) sloop *Tulip*, to begin a program of sperm whale research in the Indian Ocean Whale Sanctuary—particularly in the area off the east coast of Sri Lanka. This was the first time that such research had been attempted. Tracking groups of whales day and night by their underwater clicks, they used the small, self-sufficient vessel to locate and stay with the whales for periods of days and weeks. They identified and got to know individuals and gained unique insights into their social organization, behavior and ecology. Geographical remoteness and increasing civil strife made it impracticable to continue the research in Sri Lankan waters, so in 1985 Hal, his wife Lindy and their colleagues continued their research around the Galápagos Islands in the equatorial east Pacific. There they continue to record and unravel the complex social relationships and communication of these mysterious whales, and to throw new light on their feeding and diving behavior, and ecology. With Hal Whitehead's entry into the field, the study of sperm whales entered a new phase.

### DETERMINING AGE

Advances in research techniques and measurements have enabled scientists to determine the age of individual whales by examining and counting the growth layers in the teeth of toothed whales (top) or in the waxy earplugs of baleen whales (below).

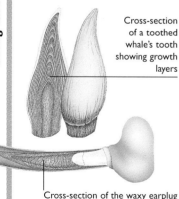

Cross-section of a toothed whale's tooth showing growth layers

Cross-section of the waxy earplug showing growth layers

**High-tech research** Although it is not unusual to find whale researchers still getting by with some fairly basic equipment, today's scientists frequently enlist the help of state-of-the-art equipment and space-age research techniques: radio transmitters, satellites in space, deep-sea submersibles, high-tech directional hydrophones, computer programs, fiber optics, deep-water video probes, DNA fingerprinting and, most recently, the United States Navy's submarine tracking system

### KNOWN FROM WHALING

Most of the information we have about sei whales comes from studies associated with whaling or whaling management. Because they prefer offshore waters, these whales are rarely seen.

is now part of the modern whale researcher's armory.

**Satellite telemetry** Unlikely as it may sound, the answers to many of the more perplexing questions about whales lie in space. Or, more precisely, they lie in satellites in

## SALT: THE MOST STUDIED WHALE IN THE WORLD

A humpback called Salt has been studied by hundreds of whale biologists and encountered by many thousands of whale watchers. Her name was derived from a distinctive white patch and a sprinkling of white spots on her dorsal fin (in the days before anyone had thought of using the black-and-white markings underneath the tail for this purpose). She was among the first of thousands of humpback whales to be identified officially. She has appeared in the Gulf of Maine in the United States every summer since she was first spotted on 1 May 1976. For several years, no one knew whether she was male or female. It was not until 1980, when she turned up with a calf by her side (later named Crystal for being a little piece of Salt) that she disclosed her well-kept secret. Salt has had many calves since, including Thalassa, Halos, Bittern and Salsa; and, in 1992, when Thalassa had a calf of her own, Salt became a grandmother for the first time. In 1978, Salt was photographed off the coast of the Dominican Republic and entered whale lore by confirming the link between the humpback feeding grounds in the Gulf of Maine and their breeding grounds 1,500 miles (2,400 km) away in the Caribbean. Biologists had suspected such a link, but Salt provided them with the first evidence, a major breakthrough in humpback whale research.

space. The idea of tracking whales by satellite has already been tried and tested on several species with considerable success. Researchers normally use a modified gun or crossbow to fire a small, battery-powered transmitter into the thick blubber of the whale's back. This beams signals up to orbiting communications satellites, which relay the coded information back to Earth. Today, in addition to signaling a whale's movements, satellite transmitters can provide a range of other information, such as swimming patterns, heart rate, and much more.

**Listening for whales** Our ability to learn about whales simply by listening to the sounds they make is no longer science fiction but scientific fact. A great deal of information can be obtained with hydrophones, which are sophisticated underwater microphones. Already, thousands of whales have been heard calling, and the experts are beginning to track their movements. It may be easier to count whales by listening to them than by looking for them. By listening carefully to the sounds whales make, it is possible to identify species, to distinguish individual animals, and to work out what they are doing.

*Sowerby's beaked whale*

# OBSERVING WHALES

Whale watching has become a global industry, but it can be enjoyed by any individual who has an elementary knowledge of whales and knows where to look. Successful whale watching requires patience. Whale watching is a time-consuming activity; it may, for example, take a whale an hour or more to pass a particular spot, but during the interval there will probably be some good photo opportunities. Other necessities include a good pair of binoculars and an awareness of prevailing weather conditions. You also need to know what species of whales are likely to occur in a particular area. To some extent this is predictable, because the migratory patterns of many species are well documented.

# PREPARING FOR FIELD TRIPS

**Whale watching requires careful preparation. Once you have decided where and when you wish to look for whales, there are a number of things to consider. Will you be on water or land? Are you going to be exposed to the elements for long periods? Will you be in a remote area?**

Wet-weather clothing

**Seasickness** If you are doing your whale watching on the water, consider whether you are prone to seasickness. If you don't know, it is safest to assume that you are. Consult your physician or pharmacist for an approved remedy, such as acupressure patches or oral medication.

**Protecting yourself** Remember that when you board a commercial whale-watching vessel,

**CHECKING FLUKES**
A reliable field guide is handy for checking out features such as the flukes of a humpback.

you should be shown what safety equipment is on board, and where it is stowed. As for protective coverings, windproof wet-weather gear and a good sunscreeen are probably the most important items, particularly if you are on the water. When dressing for cold conditions, use the "layer principle"—several relatively light layers of clothing, which trap insulating air between them. Hypothermia and sunstroke are killers, and with current levels of ozone depletion, ultraviolet radiation is a serious health risk. Good sunglasses, either polarized or UV-proof, will protect your eyes from the intense glare on the water, and also make it easier to see whales in bright conditions.

**Personal comfort** The inner person also needs looking after during long sessions searching for cetaceans. Snack food is always welcome, and cold or hot drinks may be essential in extremes of climate. Each adult will need at least

Means of protection from the sun and a flask of water are essential items of equipment.

2 pints (1 L) of fluid per day, and a good deal more in hot, dry conditions.

**Gear** The most important item is a pair of binoculars, which should always be close at hand. The magnification should be between 7 x and 10 x—the number of times closer an object appears through the binoculars than with

the naked eye. Spotting telescopes are useful, especially for land-based watching and on cruise ships, but are too powerful to keep steady on small boats. However, even on land they can't replace binoculars, and are usually used after a sighting has been made with binoculars or the naked eye. Finally, you should also have at your disposal a good field guide, such as this book, or perhaps one that specializes in the area where you are doing your whale watching.

**TELESCOPES**
Spotting telescopes are particularly good for land-based whale watching.

Binoculars

# RECORDING YOUR OBSERVATIONS

Apart from photography, there are a number of ways you can record whale-watching events: In your personal diary, keeping more detailed observations in a journal, through to keeping a computer database of your sightings. Or you may prefer to sketch or paint your subject.

**Keeping a journal** Not only is this an excellent way of remembering your sightings, it is also a very useful discipline. Your journal should be of a size that can be stored in a day-pack. It should have robust binding and, if possible, waterproof paper.

**WRITING IT DOWN**
Don't rely solely on memory. Whether you are whale watching from shore or on a boat, it is important to note down details of what you have observed.

The humble pencil (HB or softer) is the simplest and most reliable writing implement in the

outdoors—as long as you have a sharpener or a penknife at hand.

**What to record?** Every recorded sighting should be put in the context of where (either a location or a geographical position) and when (date and time) it occurred. Note what the weather and sea conditions were at the time, and if there were any other obvious features that may be associated with the sighting, such as schools of fish on the surface, large numbers of seabirds, the presence of boat traffic or predators, such as sharks.

**Points to note** Often you get only a brief glimpse of part of a whale. Training yourself to look for the presence or absence of certain

features
may help.
Such features
may include: Your
estimate of the size of a whale
relative to your boat or to some
other useful scale; the presence,
absence, size or shape of a dorsal
fin; distinctive body markings; any
visible bumps, knobs or ridges on
the top of the head; the strength,
shape and angle of the blow; and
the number of animals in a group
and whether they are close
together or spread out.

### SKETCHES

Making good sketches, as well as
written notes of sightings you have
made, can be a valuable contribution
to whale research.

**Accuracy** It is important not to
make assumptions about what you
see. Do not assume, for example,
that every whale you see during a
humpback migration is a
humpback. Simply describe what
you see—for example "three large
whales; strong, bushy blows;
obvious dorsal fins; dark color."
This may be all you have time to
notice before they disappear.

**On tape** Using a hand-held
cassette recorder to note details of
complex whale-watching events is
recommended. This is often more
convenient and quicker than
trying to commit events to paper
as they happen.

### LAPTOP CONVENIENCE

If the conditions are favorable, it
may be possible to record your
observations directly onto a laptop
computer, rather
than handwrite
them in a
notebook.

# PHOTOGRAPHING WHALES

Everyone who has photographed whales longs for a brilliant shot. A photograph of a breaching whale, for example, is a result of a combination of many things: Timing, opportunity, knowledge of how cameras and films interact, perhaps good balance—and, undoubtedly, a bit of luck.

**CAMERAS**
Zoom lenses allow considerable flexibility when your are photographing whales in the wild.

**Photographic gear** The most essential factor in obtaining good whale pictures is having the right camera gear. While poor photos can be taken with a good camera, it is very difficult to take good pictures with a poor camera.

**The right camera** Although there is an increasing variety of compact cameras, many with zoom lenses, the most suitable type for whale photography is the single-lens reflex (SLR). This camera is relatively compact, and you can change the lens to suit the situation. Alternatively, there are zoom lenses with a wide range of

**MOVEMENT ON VIDEO**
Video is a serious alternative to still photography, especially in catching scenes like porpoising dolphins, where motion is all-important. Videos also work better than still cameras in low light conditions.

**BLOWING BLUES**
The blow of the blue whale—the tallest and strongest blow of any whale—is here captured on film at fairly close quarters.

focal lengths, from wide angle to telephoto. A motor drive is a useful option when the action is fast and furious, as it often is when whales or dolphins erupt into bouts of lively activity.

**From land** Cetacean photography from land has to contend with the vagaries of weather, and requires patience, the right equipment and preparedness for the moment. You will almost certainly need a 200 mm telephoto lens or longer. However, with lenses longer than 300 mm, a tripod is essential. Early morning and late afternoon can be best for photography, unless, of course, you are shooting into glare.

**From boats and ships**
The deck of a ship can be stable but, especially on small boats, motion can be unpredictable. Find a spot where you can wedge your lower body, leaving your upper body and both hands free to weave with the boat's motion and deal with the camera. Remember that salt water is the arch enemy of camera equipment.

**FREQUENTLY FILMED**
Thrust vertically upward as the whale plunges downward, the impressive flukes of the humpback whale are among the most sought-after shots by whale-watching photographers.

# WATCHING WHALES

There's a world of whale watching to be had from land, which has the advantage of being free, and of allowing whale enthusiasts to watch independently and at any time they like. Vessel-based whale watching, on the other hand, offers an immediacy that cannot be gained on land.

**Viewing from land** The main disadvantage of shore-based whale watching is that it depends on the animals coming within viewing range, which can sometimes be frustrating. You must also be prepared to be patient and often to see nothing.

**SEEING ORCAS** In numerous locations, such as the sheltered waterways of Washington State, British Columbia, orcas may easily be observed from the shore.

**Planning encounters** There are two ways to plan your expedition. Either choose an area you wish to visit, or select a species of particular interest. Obviously, your choices are limited, as not all species closely approach land on a regular basis. Many species, such as sperm whales, are found in deep water and are usually observed from boats. Your options will also be dictated by

## HUMPBACKS

While migrating humpbacks can be observed from numerous sites on land, closer encounters from boats and ships allow much more detailed observation of humpback behavior.

the seasons, and by the seasonal movements of cetaceans themselves.

### Choosing your spot

Obviously, coastlines with high cliffs or headlands will offer the best viewing prospects. When you are viewing from a cliff top, the horizon is many times farther away than when you are viewing from sea level, and many a pleasant hour can be spent tracking the distant blows of whales as they move along a coast.

**Watching tips** Binoculars, or a spotting scope, are a must, and you will develop the knack of finding a comfortable position where you can remain for hours. Wind and sun can take their toll, so find a sheltered spot if possible. You may be able to camp at a suitable lookout. With migrating species, such as humpback and gray whales, face the direction from which the whales are likely to come, and be patient. Occasionally scan around, looking for anything out of the ordinary—a fleeting dark shape, a splash or the puff of a whale blow. Blows may be visible for 5 miles (8 km) or more through binoculars. During migrations, there may be a constant stream of whales all day, with several pods visible at once. Try to follow individual pods.

### HYDROPHONES

The calls of cetaceans are an important part of their social interactions. Many people have heard the famous songs of humpback whales, but all cetaceans "vocalize" at various times. The world of underwater sound that can be accessed by hydrophones—underwater microphones—can be a revelation. Apart from the moans, cries and clicks of cetaceans, there are the beautiful calls of seals, the snapping clicks of shrimp and the astonishing variety of sounds made by fish. You may also hear how pervasive are the sounds of boats.

The technology for listening in on whales and dolphins is simple and relatively inexpensive. Hydrophones are lowered 20–30 feet (6–9 m) into the water from a stationary boat. These are connected to a pre-amplifier, which magnifies the signal before it passes to a cassette recorder. Complete off-the-shelf units or hydrophone and pre-amp components are readily available from mail-order suppliers of electronic and scientific equipment.

### Whale watching from boats

Vessel-based whale watching includes a wide range of experiences—from paddling a kayak among whales, to spending an afternoon on a commercial whale-watching boat, to viewing them from a ferry, or the bridge of a luxury cruise liner. These experiences fall into two categories: Take yourself, or let someone else take you there.

### On your own boat

Almost any boat can be used for whale-watching. The suitability of certain types of craft depends on the location, the weather, the water conditions, the experience of the operator, and an awareness of how to behave around marine mammals. In sheltered waterways, small, fragile craft, such as sea kayaks or rowing boats, are sometimes used to approach cetaceans. Only fully proficient users of such craft should share the water with whales.

### Keeping a distance

Although whales are usually considerate toward small boats, when they are engaged in vigorous activity, such as feeding or social interaction, they may easily bump or swamp a small craft that has drifted too close. This is no time to learn self-righting techniques.

### Keeping quiet

Some vessels have less impact than others.

### FIN WHALES

Among the more commonly encountered whales in the Northern Hemisphere, fin whales can be seen close to shore off Iceland, eastern Canada, Baja California and in the Mediterranean.

Vessels under sail obviously create little underwater noise. Low-revving engines have less effect than, say, the high-pitched whine of an outboard motor at speed. Speed itself is a problem: If you are in an area frequented by marine mammals, proceed slowly and keep a sharp lookout. Also consider having a propeller guard fitted, as whales, dolphins and manatees are increasingly the victims of propeller strike.

**Competent and safe** Many people encounter whales while using small power craft, such as the runabouts used by recreational anglers. Operating any craft on open waterways is a serious undertaking, and you should not only be proficient in boat handling, but you should also be provided with suitable safety and communication equipment, and know how to use it. Warm and waterproof clothing, together with suitable food and drink, are essential items of equipment.

### Letting whales approach
Once you have sighted whales or dolphins, you must abide by the whale-watching regulations. However, there is nothing to stop whales and dolphins being drawn to you. One of the most enjoyable of whale-watching experiences is to have a vibrant group of dolphins bow riding—jostling for prime position in the wave at the bow; clicking, whistling and making eye contact with the humans peering down from just a few feet above. If you are moving at high speed, slow down as the dolphins approach. They prefer slower speeds. If you encounter whales while sailing, you may wish to heave to nearby, and wait to see if they will approach you, as they often will.

### Commercial operators
Commercial whale watching is a booming industry in many parts of the world, and has been an economic lifeline for many coastal towns, including ex-whaling communities. Most people experience their first close contact with whales through commercial operations. Most commercial operators are responsible, and have a genuine concern for the well-being of the whales. They interpret natural history and behavior for their clients. However, because whale watching has become such a competitive industry, ethics are sometimes sacrificed to gain an edge. To provide spectacular displays, such as breaching, for their customers, some operators harass whales. You can exercise responsibility by choosing an operator with a good reputation, or by pointing out any infractions that may occur.

# WHALE-WATCHING GUIDELINES

**Many countries now have whale-protection legislation in place. Guidelines designed to ensure that whales are not unduly disturbed by whale-watching activities are an important component of such legislation. These guidelines may themselves have the force of law.**

**Mutual protection** One reason that guidelines are necessary is the physical welfare of people aboard vessels, who may be at risk in situations where whales feel harassed. The main reason, however, is the welfare of the whales, because they are vulnerable to disturbance and harassment, even where it is unintended.

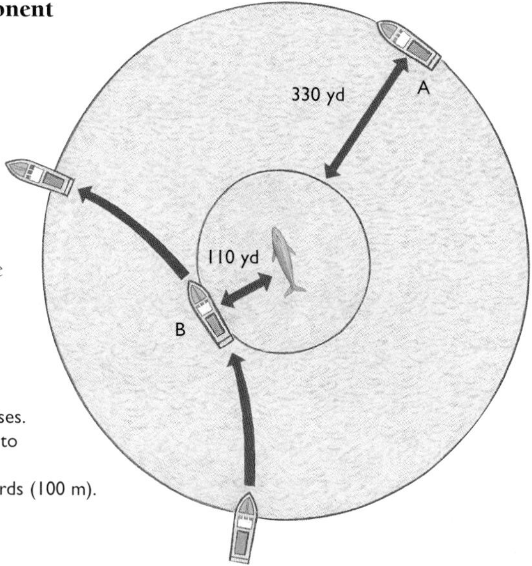

## APPROACHING A WHALE

When approaching a whale in a boat, avoid making loud noises. Either (A) position your craft 330 yards (300 m) ahead and to one side of the animal and wait quietly for it to pass, or (B) approach slowly from the side, never closer than 110 yards (100 m). Swimmers should leave 33 yards (30 m) clear. (This illustration is not to scale.)

330 yd   A

110 yd

B

**Underwater sounds** Whales are vulnerable to harassment by sounds. Sound travels much faster and farther through water than in air. Many vessels produce engine or propeller noises that at close range could disturb many species.

Just as important, some frequencies are more of a problem than others, depending on the hearing and vocal ranges of the species concerned.

**Physical intrusion** The very presence of boats within or near a group of whales, or even a single whale, can disrupt their normal activities. Whales and dolphins live their lives according to strict time and energy budgets and, often, can ill afford to be distracted from vital behaviors, such as breeding, feeding or nursing calves, to avoid craft that may be disturbing them.

**Polite distances** Boats can physically threaten whales by violating "polite" distances, or they can separate whales from others in the pod, which is particularly serious in the case of mothers and calves. Low-flying aircraft, particularly helicopters, may appear threatening to cetaceans and cause them distress. At the first sign of disturbance, such as an unusual or abrupt change in behavior, you should back off immediately.

**KEEP YOUR DISTANCE**
Amateur whale watchers should never venture too close to the mighty tail of a diving humpback.

# OBSERVATION TECHNIQUES

Finding whales at sea is quite a challenge, but with practice, patience and a little luck anyone can do it. The first step is to work out exactly where to look. This could be near the coast, over an underwater canyon or seamount, on the edge of a continental shelf, near an estuary, or anywhere else that seems appropriate for the species you are hoping to find.

**How to look**  When it comes to the search itself, you can either move around haphazardly, following hunches, or take a more scientific approach and use transects (pre-planned routes along a grid system). Both methods work with varying degrees of success. Whale scientists prefer transects, especially when they are conducting an official survey, because this system gives directly comparable results from survey to survey. But whichever system you choose, try not to be in too much of a hurry. The number of whales you see tends to be in inverse proportion to the speed of the vessel. So take your time and search properly.

### ASYMMETRY
At sea, the fin whale is most likely to be confused with blue and sei whales. All others are much smaller. However, the fin whale has a dramatic color asymmetry which whale watchers may observe: white on the lower right side of the head; black on the lower left.

### EASY TO RECOGNIZE

Orcas (above) can be observed in all oceans of the world, from the poles to the tropics. They are most likely to be found, however, in cooler coastal areas, where their selected prey species are most abundant. They are easily identified by their size—they are the largest of all dolphins—and by their distinctive markings: white eye patch, gray saddle patch and black back. These very inquisitive dolphins frequently come up to boats to inspect them and often indulge in greatly entertaining and vigorous displays of activity.

**What to look for**  People who have spent a lot of time looking for whales and dolphins instinctively recognize the tiniest clues. With large whales, it is normally the blow, which is often very distinctive. Alternatively, you may just see the whale's back breaking the surface, or its tail raised briefly before a dive. It often resembles a strange wave that does not look quite right, so anything suspicious is worth taking the time to investigate further. Splashes are also telltale signs. They can be caused by breaching, flipper-slapping and lobtailing whales, or by a distant school of dolphins, which can look like just a rough patch of water. The presence of birds can be another useful clue, especially if they are concentrated in a small area, or seem to be feeding. It could mean that there are a lot of fish in the water and whales and dolphins are feeding from underneath.

### BELUGAS

Only whale watchers prepared to brave the rigors of Arctic and subarctic waters can expect to see these robust and blubbery whales in the wild. The best place to find them is in shallow bays and estuaries during the Arctic summer.

# IDENTIFICATION TECHNIQUES

Identifying cetaceans at sea can be frustratingly difficult, and even the world's experts are unable to identify every animal they encounter. Developing the the skills necessary to tell the species apart can be satisfying, but the animals do not make it easy.

**Hard to see** Whales spend most of their time hidden from view underwater, and even when they come to the surface to breathe, they often disappear before it is possible to get a good look. When they do reveal more of themselves, or stay on the surface for longer, many of them look remarkably similar and are almost impossible to tell apart. There is even a great deal of variation within each species, and no two individuals look exactly alike: They vary in color and behave differently, and their dorsal fins are not uniform.

**More complications** The simple fact that whales and dolphins live in the sea adds yet more complications. Imagine trying to get an accurate impression of an animal on the move, while struggling to keep your balance on a rolling, slippery deck. Adverse conditions, such as whitecaps, high winds, heavy swell, driving rain, or even glare from the sun, add to the challenge.

**Common species** Despite all these potential difficulties though, there are ways of identifying

**FLIPPER BANDING**
A good way to identify a minke whale is to look for the white band on the pectoral fins. You won't always see it, however, because in some places minkes' pectoral fins are all black.

whales, dolphins and porpoises. In fact, it is quite possible for anyone to recognize the relatively common and distinctive species and, eventually, many of the more unusual ones as well. All that is required is a little background knowledge and some practice.

### HEAVILY SCARRED

Risso's dolphin is easy to identify at close quarters. It is heavily scarred, ghostlike and looks like no other species. From a distance, however, the tall, curved-back dorsal fin could be confused with that of an orca or a bottlenose dolphin. Risso's dolphin is the largest cetacean to bear the name "dolphin."

**Elimination** The best approach is to use a relatively simple process of elimination. Run through a mental checklist of key features when a new animal is encountered at sea. The more features you are able to take into account, the better chance you have of making a positive identification. Ultimately, the process becomes automatic, and you learn to recognize a species by its unique combination

### EASY TO IDENTIFY

Identifying short-finned pilot whales is fairly easy. They sometimes travel with dolphins, but they are much larger and their black bodies are darker—most dolphins tend to be gray. The short-finned pilot whale's dorsal fin is broad-based and set far forward on the back.

of features, or, in bird-watching jargon, its own "jizz," a slang term for "general impression of size and shape."

255

# IDENTIFICATION SKILLS

Whale biologists and expert naturalists on whale-watch tours somehow seem able to identify every fleeting blow, fin, back or tail they see—merely at a glance. So what is their secret? The following will give you some clues and advice about how to improve your identification skills and so become able to make more frequent positive identifications.

**Jumping to conclusions** The first rule of whale identification is: Never jump to conclusions. Professional whale scientists don't, and whale watchers shouldn't, because it does little to improve identification skills. It is perfectly acceptable to record simply "unidentified dolphin" or "unidentified whale," if it is not possible to make a more accurate identification.

**DIFFERING FLUKES**
A humpback's flukes (above) are usually easy to distinguish from those of a gray whale (left). The humpback's flukes have a mixed black-and-white pattern, which can vary from almost completely white, with black markings, to almost completely black, with white markings. The gray whale's flukes are, like the rest of its body, a mottled gray. In both pictures, the whales are lobtailing—slapping the flukes against the surface of the water while most of the animal remains below the surface. Lobtailing is sometimes a response to harassment.

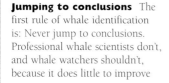

## IDENTIFICATION CHECKLIST

**Geographical location** There are not many places in the world with records of more than a few dozen species of whales, dolphins and porpoises. So taking the location into account immediately limits the number of possibilities.

**Habitat** Just as woodpeckers inhabit woodlands rather than shores, and giant pandas prefer mountains to wetlands, most whales, dolphins and porpoises are adapted to specific marine or freshwater habitats.

**Unusual features** The tall dorsal fin of the male orca, the long tusk of the male narwhal, the extraordinary curved teeth of the male strap-toothed whale and highly distinctive features of some other species can often be useful for a quick identification.

**Size** Estimating size at sea is difficult, unless a direct comparison can be made with the length of the boat or something else in the water. But simply deciding whether the animal is small, medium or large can help to eliminate a range of possibilities.

**Color and markings** Distinctive markings and bright colors can be useful identification features. However, since colors at sea vary according to water clarity and light conditions, they can also be quite confusing if they are at all subtle.

**Dorsal fin** The size, shape and position of the dorsal fin varies greatly among species and a few species have no fin at all. Such details can be useful in combination with other features for making a positive identification.

**Flippers** It is rarely possible to see the flippers, or pectoral fins, clearly—but their length, color, shape, and their position on the animal's body, vary greatly from one species to another.

**Body shape** The animal's overall shape can sometimes be useful, although many whales, dolphins and porpoises rarely show enough of themselves to give a satisfactory impression.

**Beak** In oceanic dolphins, and some other whales, the presence or absence of a beak is a very useful identification feature.

**Flukes** Some large whales lift the flukes high into the air before a dive; others do not. This distinction alone can help with identification, but it is also worth checking the shape of the flukes, which vary considerably from species to species.

**Blow or spout** The blow is immensely useful for identifying larger whales. It varies in height, shape and visibility among species and, especially on calm days, can be all that is needed for a positive identification.

**Dive sequence** The way in which a whale, dolphin or porpoise breaks the surface to breathe, and then dives again, is known as its dive sequence. In some species, this is very distinctive, although differences in others can be quite subtle.

**Behavior** Most whales, dolphins and porpoises have been known to breach, pec-slap, lobtail and perform other such behaviors at one time or another. But they all have slightly different techniques, and some are more active at the surface than others.

**Group size** The number of animals seen together is a useful indicator; some species are highly gregarious, while others tend to live alone or in small groups.

**Keeping notes** Having logged your sightings as "unidentified," it is important to write notes. As well as helping to improve your field skills, taking notes may help you to make a positive identification if you see the same species again, even if it is months later. Better still, it may help you to identify the animal at home, where you can consult field guides and other reference works.

**The sooner the better** The sooner you write notes, the better. It is amazing how quickly many of the more subtle details of a sighting are forgotten, even just minutes after a whale or dolphin has disappeared into the murky depths. Run through the list of identification features set out on the previous page, from the dive sequence to the shape of the beak, and then make a note of the time, date, location, weather and sea conditions, as well as any other details that might be relevant.

**More rather than less** At first, it is better to err on the side of making too many notes, even if you seem to be spending more of your time writing about the whales than observing them. After a little practice, of course, it will become easier to decide what you should or should not include. But never stop writing or sketching altogether. Even as you become more proficient at whale identification, it is still worth jotting down useful details. They all help to build up a more complete picture of the species you see regularly. You could include photos and other mementos to turn your journal into a permanent record of the sightings you have made.

**Learning from the experts** Reading books, watching films about whales, studying photos, and even sharpening your powers of observation on local wildlife, will all help to hone your identification skills. But there is no real substitute for whale watching

*Minke whale*

with an expert. This is why it is so important to select whale-watching tours with knowledgeable biologists or naturalists on board. Listen to the commentaries and don't by shy about asking questions—most people working on whale-watch boats enjoy talking about whales and welcome questions from anyone who displays a genuine interest.

**A feel for the "jizz"** After a while, it will become clear that people who spend a lot of time around cetaceans develop a feel for the "jizz," or general impression, of different species. We recognize our friends and relatives instinctively because of an undefinable combination of some or all of their features. With wildlife, using the jizz is not always a foolproof system—and it is no substitute for checking the details later—but it is definitely a technique worth taking the trouble to master. Becoming proficient at identifying whales is much like any other skill. It takes time, perseverance and practice. At the end of the day, it is all about an attitude of mind—watching inquisitively, listening carefully, writing notes properly and identifying cautiously.

#### HEADS AND MOUTHS
The shape of the head and the features of the mouth are a useful guide to the identification of numerous species of whales, dolphins and porpoises.

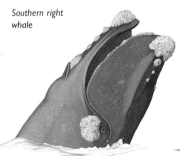

*Southern right whale*

*Sperm whale*

*Bottlenose dolphin*

# WHALE-WATCHING SITES

The special fascination that humans feel for whales and the thrill of seeing these often awesome, and frequently entertaining, creatures in their natural environment have made whale watching a favorite pastime for millions of people right throughout the world. Indeed, a global industry has developed from this activity. One of the best and most educative ways to observe whales is to go on one or more of the whale-watching cruises or tours that operate in places all around the world, even in previously inaccessible Arctic and Antarctic regions. Many of these tours employ qualified guides or naturalists to provide background information and interpret whale behavior.

261

# WHERE TO OBSERVE WHALES

Opportunities to watch and learn about cetaceans and their habitats and behavior are offered in key areas of the world, from the Arctic to Antarctica. In whatever country you live, there are likely to be places not too far distant where you can take the opportunity to observe whales at close quarters.

**Whale-watching regions** The following pages feature 30 special areas, which are divided into 7 regions, all of which are reliable places to watch whales, dolphins and porpoises. Each of the regions is introduced with a general overview of the area, tracing the way in which whale watching developed there and presenting key facts about the region and the whales that you can encounter there. For each region a map indicates the location of each of the sites that follows.

**Facts and figures** Each site in each of the seven regions is dealt with in turn under the headings "When to visit," "Weather," "Types of tours," "Tours available" and "Special features." These entries provide an invaluable guide for the intending whale watcher, giving vital information that will help you get the most out of your whale-watching excursion. They set out clearly the species of whales you can expect to see and the times of year each species is likely to be in the area.

**CETACEAN VIEWING SITES**
1   Southeast Alaska
2   British Columbia and Puget Sound
3   California, Oregon and Washington
4   Baja California
5   Hawaii
6   St. Lawrence River and the Gulf
7   The Maritimes and Newfoundland
8   New England
9   Florida and the Bahamas
10  The Caribbean
11  Ecuador and Colombia
12  Brazil and the Amazon River
13  Argentina
14  Iceland
15  Norway
16  Greenland and the Faeroe Islands
17  Britain and Ireland
18  The Mediterranean
19  Canaries and Azores
20  South Africa and Madagascar
21  South Asia
22  Japan: Ogasawara and Okinawa
23  Japan: Kochi Prefecture
24  East Coast Australia
25  Southern Australia
26  Western Australia
27  New Zealand
28  Tonga and other Pacific Islands
29  The Arctic
30  Antarctica

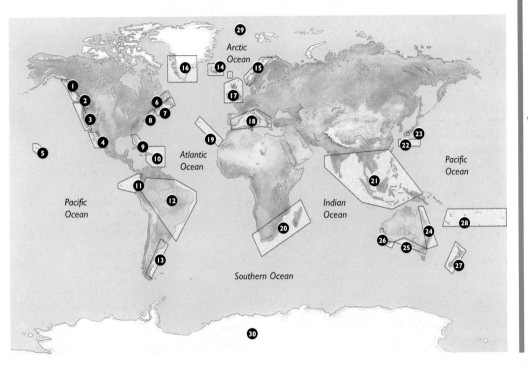

# WEST COAST OF NORTH AMERICA

**Home of the earliest whale-watch tours, the west coast of North America offers excellent opportunities to sight a wide diversity of cetaceans. The world's first commercial whale watching occurred in southern California in early 1955, when Chuck Chamberlain, a fisherman from San Diego, put out a sign that said, simply, "See the Whales—$1."**

**Gray whales** The whales that Chamberlain's sign referred to were gray whales that migrated along the west coast of North America every winter. The trips proved a steady seller and, four years later, Raymond M. Gilmore, a marine scientist, began the first trips to be led by a naturalist. By the late 1960s, Gilmore and others were leading trips to Baja California to encounter the gray whales mating and raising their calves in Scammon's Lagoon. Soon the whale-watching craze spread north and south along the coast.

**The end of whaling** In the early 1970s, as whaling finally came to a halt around North America and whales started returning to coastal waters, more than 20 fishing and other communities became involved in whale watching, which became a way of life for those who fished or worked in the travel industry to earn some money during winter.

**Farther afield** Whale watching spread steadily on the west coast and soon spread to Hawaii. At first, humpback tours were conducted from Lahaina, on Maui, but today tours leave from all the main islands and encounter

## SUCCESS STORIES

Some of the species seen along the West Coast are conservation success stories, notably the gray whale, which was declared a protected species, with some protected habitat, and is now thriving. Fortunately, the pressure of human population is not as severe here as on the United States east coast, the St. Lawrence and in Europe.

a variety of tropical dolphins, as well as the humpbacks. Alaska joined the ranks, with humpbacks again the main attraction. In British Columbia, the orcas became the first toothed whales to be commercially watched, and trips to see them soon rivaled the popularity of tours to observe some of the large baleen whales.

**A widening repertoire** In the late 1970s seabird and other tours to the waters off San Francisco and Monterey, California, began turning up some amazing finds from August to October: blue and humpback whales, and a wide assortment of other species. As the whale-watching business flourished, these important areas for whales, birds and fish soon became candidates to be declared marine-protected zones. At the same time, the Gulf of California, between Baja California and mainland Mexico, became the site for watching a wide variety of whales, including blue, humpback, Bryde's, fin and minke, as well as dolphins. Opportunites for whale watching along the Pacific coast are among the most diverse and of the highest quality in the world. Most whales and dolphins can be seen close to shore, but the ports vary in their accessibility.

Southeast Alaska

British Columbia

Pacific Ocean

California, Oregon and Washington

Baja California

**Whale-Watching Sites**

### Southeast Alaska

*When to visit* June–early Sept: humpbacks, minke whales, orcas, Pacific white-sided dolphins, Dall's and harbor porpoises. Bubblenetting humpbacks best in June–early July.

*Weather* June–Sept: cool to cold on the water and weather subject to extreme and sudden changes, including onset of fog and rain. August is the prime month for weather, seas and whales.

*Types of tours* Multi-day cruises on small and large cruise ships and kayak expeditions; day trips on fishing, sail, inflatable and whale-watch boats.

*Tours available* Gustavus, Pt. Adolphus, Glacier Bay, Ketchikan, Juneau, Petersburg, Elfin Cove, Wrangell Island, Sitka; also long-range cruise ships from Seattle, Vancouver, Prince Rupert, San Francisco.

*Special features* Alaska is a major cruise ship destination. Today many cruise ships take a few hours, or even schedule a half-day excursion, to spend time with the whales, usually in Icy Strait, near Gustavus, and Glacier Bay. Wildlife watching is a big part of all tours to southeast Alaska. Besides the high-profile humpback whales and orcas, you can see harbor seals and Steller sea lions on remote rocky islets. Southeast Alaska has the highest density of black bears in the world. To see black bears and eagles feeding on spawning salmon in the rivers, the Pack Creek Cooperative Management Area/Stan Price Wildlife Sanctuary has camping and guided tours in July and August.

**IDYLLIC SCENE**
The picturesque waters of Puget Sound, at the very northeast corner of the United States, are a favorite destination for whale watchers.

## British Columbia and Puget Sound

*When to visit* Mar–Apr: gray whales (west Vancouver Island); May–Sept orcas, Pacific white-sided dolphins, Dall's porpoises (north Vancouver Island), harbor porpoises (south Vancouver Island), gray whales (west Vancouver Island).

*Weather* Mar–June: often rainy and cold on water; July–Aug: cool on water but usually dry, fog especially mornings on west coast Vancouver Island.

*Types of tours* Half- and full-day tours, multi-day expeditions; inflatables, sailboats and large whale-watch boats; some whale watching from ferries.

*Tours available* British Columbia: Alert Bay, Telegraph Cove, Port McNeill, Sointula, Tofino, Ucluelet, Victoria, Nanaimo; Puget Sound area: Anacortes, Bellingham, Friday Harbor, Seattle.

*Special features* Harbor seals and California and Steller sea lions can be seen on rocky islets along the coast. The most accessible locales are Race Rocks at the southern tip of Vancouver Island and Sea Lion Rocks off Long Beach in the Pacific Rim National Park. In many other spots along the coast of Vancouver Island, bald eagles prey on salmon and other fish species.

**ON PATROL**
Orcas patrol the straits and island passages off the coast of southeast Alaska in pods of 10 or more. They are there to feed on salmon, although other orcas, the so-called "transients," come to feed on porpoises, seals and other marine mammals, which sometimes include whales. Judging from the orca teeth marks on many humpback whale tails, they try, but are rarely successful in making a kill.

### California, Oregon and Washington

*When to visit* Dec–May: migrating gray whales; June–Sept: summering gray whales, north California to Washington; Aug–Oct blue, humpback and other whales and dolphins off the coast of central California.

*Weather* June–Sept: cool to cold on water, even when hot on land; Oct–May: California to Washington, cold, rainy.

*Types of tours* Half- and full-day tours, multi-day expeditions; inflatables, fishing, sail and large whale-watch boats.

*Tours available* California: Avila Beach, Balboa, Dana Point, El Granada, Fort Bragg, Hollister, La Mesa, Long Beach, Monterey, Morro Bay, Oceanside, Oxnard, Point Arena, Redondo Beach, San Diego, San Pedro, Santa Barbara, Santa Cruz, Ventura; Oregon: Charleston, Depoe Bay, Garibaldi, Newport; Washington (west coast only): La Push, Neah Bay, Westport

*Special features* In the late 1970s, dedicated seabird cruises, taken during August to October to the offshore canyons and banks west

**COMMON ENCOUNTERS**
Pacific white-sided dolphins are commonly encountered on whale-watching tours off all parts of the United States west coast. These inquisitive dolphins often approach boats to inspect them at close quarters. Their vigorous activities ensure that they often steal the show on off-shore whale-watch trips.

of San Francisco and Monterey, began to encounter dolphins and a variety of whales, such as blues and humpbacks. In all, there have been sightings of 26 cetacean species, almost a third of all species, including sporadic sightings of a number of rare beaked whales.

## SUMMER AND FALL SIGHTINGS

Northern right whale dolphins can often be seen, traveling in groups of between 5 and 200 individuals, on late summer and fall whale-watch tours to the Monterey marine canyon, California. They sometimes treat whale watchers to graceful displays of bow riding. Until the mid-1970s, when cetacean biologists Stephen Leatherwood and William A. Walker began to study them, this species was considered rare.

## CHRISTMAS TREATS

About Christmastime every year, humpback whales return to sing, fight, mate and raise their calves in the tropical blue waters off Hawaii. Humpbacks make their winter homes near these islands. Migrating from Alaska, the female humpbacks often arrive first, some heavy with calf, others having just given birth. The males arrive later in search of a partner.

### Baja California

*When to visit* Jan–Apr: gray whales live in the lagoons of Baja California, and blue, Bryde's, humpback, fin and minke whales move into the Gulf of California; year-round, Pacific white-sided, common and various tropical dolphins, bottlenose dolphins (in gray whale lagoons and in the Gulf of California).

*Weather* Dry, clear, warm winters; wind, especially on the Pacific side, can make it cool at sea.

*Types of tours* Multi-day expeditions, some day trips; inflatables, pangas, sailboats, medium-size cruise ships.

*Tours available* La Paz, Ensenada, Tijuana, Rosarito, San Diego.

*Special features* In 1993, Mexico's newest reserve, the Upper Gulf of California and Colorado River Delta Biosphere Reserve, was established to protect the vaquita, the small, endangered porpoise that lives only in this part of the world. You may not spot a vaquita, but, as compensation, humpbacks are sometimes encountered and fin whales are often seen.

**FRIENDLY BUT FRIGHTENING**
Friendly gray whales often approach whale-watching boats off the coast of Baja California. Occasionally they may gently nudge a boat, or even ease it up and out of the water, which can be a memorable, if rather nerve-racking, experience for whale watchers.

## Hawaii

*When to visit*  Late Dec–Apr: for humpback whales, largest concentrations in Feb and Mar; year-round: spinner, bottlenose, and pantropical spotted dolphins, false killer whales, short-finned pilot whales and many others.

*Weather*  Warm to hot; sometimes strong Kona winds bring rain and high seas.

*Types of tours*  Half- and full-day tours, some extended multi-day expeditions; inflatables, sailboats and large whale-watch boats.

*Tours available*  Maui: Lahaina, Kihei, Maalaea; Hawaii (big island): Keauhou, Kailua-Kona, Kohala Coast, Honokoha; Oahu: Honolulu, Kaneohe. Kauai: Hanalei.

*Special features*  From the main street of Lahaina, signs of whale-watching culture date from the 1970s. In front of the Pioneer Hotel, once home to whaling captains waiting for South Seas postings, about 20 whale-watch boards are berthed, each with its signboard displayed. Key features to look for when choosing a whale-watch tour are an on-board naturalist or nature guide and a boat equipped with hydrophones, through which you can hear the haunting songs of humpbacks.

**SANDY SHORELINE**
The sandy shoreline of Hanalei Bay, on the northern coast of the Hawaiian island of Kauai. Hanalei is a popular starting point for whale-watching tours.

271

# EAST COAST OF NORTH AMERICA

**The first commercial whale watching on the east coast of North America occurred in Canada in 1971, when a summer trip by members of the Zoological Society of Montreal took them down the St. Lawrence River to see belugas and some large baleen whales.**

**Growing interest** This first commercial excursion was so successful that more trips were soon organized. In 1975, the Dolphin Fleet of Provincetown, Massachusetts, entered the whale-watch business, based largely on humpback whales, and the idea spread up the coast of Maine to the Canadian Maritime provinces and Newfoundland. By the late 1980s, the success of whale watching on the North American east coast eclipsed that of the West Coast in terms of numbers, and this area now leads the world with more than 1.5 million people whale watching there every year.

**Spreading southward**
Most of the activity in northeast North America is centered around the feeding grounds of large baleen whales from May to November. It was partly the search by scientists for the mating and calving grounds of some of these whales that led to whale watching in the Caribbean from January to April. In the early 1980s, trips to see Atlantic spotted dolphins had started in the Bahamas, off Florida—the first commercial tours anywhere to offer a chance to swim with wild dolphins. In 1986, the Silver Bank Humpback Whale Sanctuary, north of the Dominican Republic, was established.

### HUMAN IMPACT

Although the proximity of large population centers has had advantages for whale conservation, it has also had a more adverse impact on cetaceans in the form of shipping traffic, marine pollution and other human-related factors. Great care will be needed to manage whale watching and protect the habitat to ensure that cetaceans and humans have a shared future to enjoy.

### Commerce and science

Throughout the region, science and education have gone hand in hand with commercial whale-watching development—more so than anywhere else in the world. Photo-identification studies have produced excellent records and catalogs, and databases of sightings have been set up for each baleen whale species in the North Atlantic. If researchers in the Caribbean encounter a certain humpback mother and her newborn calf, researchers in New England might photograph them a few months later when the whales come north to feed, documenting the growing calf until it is time to move south again. Over several years, behavioral portraits of individual animals have emerged, as well as precise records of movements, associations, entanglements in nets and other life events.

### Easy access

Whale watching on the east coast of North America has benefited from the fact that there is easy access to most sites from large cities. The popularity of the whales has helped with conservation measures, such as the designation of a marine-protected area at Stellwagen Bank, off Massachusetts.

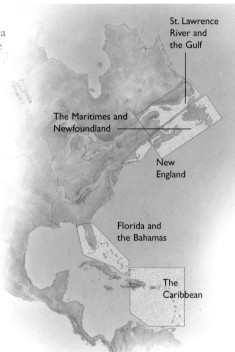

St. Lawrence River and the Gulf

The Maritimes and Newfoundland

New England

Florida and the Bahamas

The Caribbean

273

## St. Lawrence River and the Gulf

*When to visit* St. Lawrence at Saguenay River: June–Nov fin, minke whales, belugas, harbor porpoises; Les Escoumins to Pointe-des-Monts, river and north shore of gulf, especially Mingan Islands: June– Nov: blue, fin, minke, humpback whales, occasional orcas, Atlantic white-sided dolphins and harbor porpoises in Aug–Nov.

*Weather* July–Sept: cool to cold on the water, fog common, some heavy summer rains, snow by mid-Oct or Nov.

*Types of tours* Half- and full-day tours, some extended multi-day expeditions; inflatables, sailboats and large whale-watch boats; good land-based whale watching.

*Tours available* St. Lawrence River, Quebec: Tadoussac, Baie-Ste-Catherine, Grandes-Bergeronnes, Les Escoumins, Godbout, Baie-Comeau, Baie-Trinité, Pointe-des-Monts; Gulf of St. Lawrence, Quebec: Longue-Pointe-de-Mingan, Havre-Saint-Pierre; Gaspé Peninsula: Rivière-du-Renard, Gaspé.

### ST. LAWRENCE ICE FLOES
Whales arrive in the St. Lawrence River soon after the winter ice thaws and the river becomes navigable.

*Special features* Where the St. Lawrence and Saguenay rivers meet is the southernmost area in the world to see belugas. They can be sighted from the lookout at Pointe Noire or during tours that depart from Tadoussac. The boats don't target the belugas, since they are endangered. They are likely to be seen only at some distance. The image of their ghostly white bodies, however, leaves a lasting impression, and if the boat carries a hydrophone, there's a chance of hearing their constant sounds. Now reduced to about 500 from a population of several thousand, the St. Lawrence belugas have had to endure contaminants and pesticides from heavy industrial use of the river system, including extensive shipping traffic and effluent outflows upstream from large United States and Canadian cities on the Great Lakes. Every year numbers of belugas are found

## RUGGED COASTLINE

Waves lash the rocky coastline of Newfoundland in eastern Canada. This coast has sheer coastal cliffs from which the whale watcher can view fantastic seabird colonies and abundant whales that come in close to shore.

stranded and are examined by a dedicated research team. But there are still some new calves appearing every year, and the youngsters, bluish gray beside their white mothers, occasionally poke their heads out of the water.

**SUMMER VISITORS**
Fin whales are one of numerous whale species that come to the waters off New England and use the area as a summer feeding ground.

lies the Gully, a deep canyon. This is the only known place where northern bottlenose whales can reliably be seen.

## The Maritimes and Newfoundland
*When to visit*  June–Oct: fin, humpback, minke whales, various dolphins and harbor porpoises; Aug–early Nov: northern right whales, Bay of Fundy and off Nova Scotia.
*Weather*  June–Aug: cool to cold; fog especially in Bay of Fundy; Sept–Oct: colder but often clearer.
*Types of tours*  Half- and full-day tours, extended multi-day expeditions; inflatables, sailboats, whale-watch boats; some whale watching from ferries.
*Tours available*  New Brunswick: Grand Manan, Leonardville, Fredericton; Nova Scotia: Halifax, Tiverton, Westport (Brier Island), Cheticamp, Capstick; Newfoundland: St. John's, Bay Bulls, Trinity, Twillingate.
*Special features*  About 100 miles (160 km) out to sea in the North Atlantic, off eastern Nova Scotia,

## New England
*When to visit*  Apr–May: right, minke, humpback, fin and small cetaceans; June–Oct: all whales are common, except right whales, which are seen only occasionally; Aug–Oct: northern right whales off northeast Maine from Lubec.
*Weather*  Warm to hot, especially from Massachusetts ports May–Aug; it can be cool out on the sea; rain is most likely in Apr–early May.

encounters with whales, sightings of some 40 species of resident marine birds, including loons, storm petrels and shearwaters.

### BOTTLENOSE

Northern bottlenose whales (left) are the prize residents of, and the most commonly seen whales in the Gully, a deep canyon off eastern Nova Scotia. The Florida Keys (below) provide some excellent sites for shore-based watching of bottlenose dolphins.

*Types of tours* Half- and full-day boat trips; some extended multi-day trips; large whale-watch boats.

*Tours available* Massachusetts: Provincetown, Nantucket, Barnstable, Plymouth, Boston, Gloucester, Newburyport; New Hampshire: Rye, Hampton Beach, Portsmouth; Maine: Bar Harbor, Kennebunkport, Lubec, Northeast Harbor, Ogunquit, Portland, Boothbay Harbor.

*Special features* The Stellwagen Bank National Marine Sanctuary offers, as well as

### Florida and the Bahamas

*When to visit* For Atlantic spotted and bottlenose dolphins year-round; May–Sept best for Bahamas. Check hurricane reports June–Oct.

*Weather* Warm to hot, generally calm during May–Sept.

*Types of tours* Mainly 3–11 day expeditions to Bahamas (book in advance); some day tours in Florida waters; inflatables, sailboats, motor cruisers and dive boats.

*Tours available* Florida: Key West; Florida to Bahamas: Jupiter, Dania, Fort Lauderdale, Indialantic, Miami Beach; Bahamas: West End, Port Lucaya, Freeport (Grand Bahama Island).

*Special features* For the past few years, a number of special one-week marine mammal survey expeditions have been offered through Earthwatch.

**IDEAL AND IDYLLIC**
The idyllic, clear waters of the Caribbean are an ideal location for observing a wide variety of whale and dolphin species.

## The Caribbean

*When to visit* Jan–Apr: humpback whales; year-round: sperm whales and various dolphins; inquire locally, as tour operating seasons vary (for example, St. Vincent, dolphins, Apr–Sept).

*Weather* Warm to hot, seas sometimes rough; tours often confine activities to the lee side of islands. Storms sometimes Aug–Oct; rainy season varies, but seasonal daily rain may last for

### GRENADA

Grenada in the Caribbean has several dolphin-watch operators who take visitors to see bottlenose dolphins (left) as well as spinner and spotted dolphins.

only part of a day.

*Types of tours* Half- and full-day tours, some extended multi-day expeditions in Dominican Republic; inflatables, sailboats and large whale-watch boats.

*Tours available* Dominican Republic: Samaná, Puerto Plata, Santo Domingo; Puerto Rico: Rincon; US Virgin Islands: Long Bay, St. Thomas; British Virgin Islands: Road Town, Tortola; Guadeloupe: Le Moule; Dominica: Roseau; Martinique: Carbet; St. Vincent: Arnos

Vale; Grenada: St. George's, Carriacou (Grenadines).

*Special features* Since the early 1990s, Paul Knapp Jr. has invited several hundred people each winter to listen to male humpback whales singing in the waters north of Tortola. Visitors concentrate on sounds delivered by high-quality hydrophones and speakers.

### HUMPBACKS

Every year, from January to April some 3,000 humpbacks gather in the warm-water setting of the Caribbean.

# SOUTH AMERICA

**South America has everything from river dolphins deep in the jungle to the great southern right whales off Patagonia. Commercial whale-watching tours in South America started in Argentina in 1983. As early as 1970, Roger Payne began his photo-identification work on southern right whales at Península Valdés, Patagonia.**

**Patagonia** Many whale and dolphin researchers from around the world made treks to this area through the 1970s and early 1980s, and their fascinating stories of Patagonia and the whales and dolphins living in the sheltered bays of the peninsula spread worldwide.

**Other sites** Even before whale study and research began in Patagonia, cetacean watching was a part of jungle excursions to the Amazon as well as boat tours around the Galápagos Islands. But the success of whale watching in Argentina has led to the expansion of dolphin watching along the coast of Brazil and in the Amazon basin, and the introduction of new whale-watch tours along the coasts of both Ecuador and Colombia. All the other countries in South America, except land-locked Paraguay, have some whale-watching activity, and even where there are no commercial tours, there are still viewing opportunities from land. Wherever you go, along the coast and up the rivers, keep your eyes open.

**Migrating whales** Many of the large whales are visitors to South America. They spend part of the year feeding in the Antarctic waters and then swim north to

---

**SOUTHERN SOUTH AMERICA**
Southern South America has a great diversity of unusual species: At least six dolphins and porpoises are found mainly or only in these waters, especially off Chile or Argentina. As well, some of the rarer beaked whales are seeen in the offshore waters or stranded on the beaches of this region, including two new species of beaked whale described as recently as the early 1990s.

warmer climates, heading either east or west of Tierra del Fuego to reach the South Pacific or the South Atlantic. In most cases the migration stops before the Equator, but some humpbacks cross the Equator and move as far north as Colombia and Costa Rica—the longest migration by an individual whale that has so far been documented.

**Visitors and residents** Waters around South America provide mating, calving and nursery grounds for the large whales, while the smaller whales and dolphins live here year-round and find their food and mates in the same waters, with no need to migrate.

**Access** Access to whale watching in parts of South America is more difficult than in North America and some other parts of the world. But the thrill of seeing river dolphins, the big southern rights or rare dolphins in or around the Strait of Magellan make this a unique and interesting region to visit.

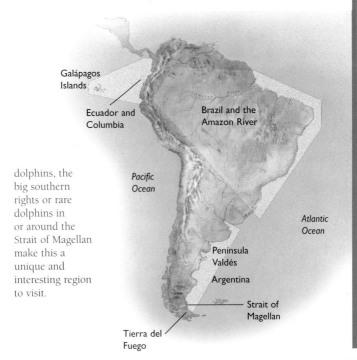

Galápagos Islands

Ecuador and Columbia

Brazil and the Amazon River

Pacific Ocean

Atlantic Ocean

Península Valdés

Argentina

Strait of Magellan

Tierra del Fuego

# SOUTH AMERICA continued

### Ecuador and Colombia

*When to visit* Year-round: bottlenose, pantropical spotted and other dolphins Ecuador and Galápagos; offshore Ecuador: spinner dolphins, orcas, sperm and Bryde's whales; humpback whales June–Sept Ecuador, and Aug–Oct Colombia.

*Weather* Coastal Ecuador and Colombia hot, humid year-round, sometimes rainy during humpback whale season; the Galápagos are drier, best months for sea conditions Mar–Aug, although year-round possible.

*Types of tours* Half- and full-day tours, extended multi-day expeditions; inflatables, sailboats, small motorboats and small cruise ships.

*Tours available* Ecuador: Guayaquil, Quito, Machalilla National Park, Puerto López, Salango; Colombia: Cali, Buenaventura, Bahía, Juanchaco, Ladrilleros, Bahía Solano, El Valle, Chocó.

*Special features* Today, all the waters around the Galápagos are a whale and dolphin sanctuary. Bottlenose, common and spinner dolphins can be seen close to shore, while sperm and Bryde's whales are farther offshore.

### Brazil and the Amazon River

*When to visit* Year-round: river dolphins in Amazon–Orinoco but best during low-water seasons as dolphins are more confined, and you avoid rainy season; tucuxi dolphins at Santa Catarina Island,

**ROCKY ISLANDS**
The rugged shores and offshore waters of the Galápagos Islands harbor an incomparable wealth of wildlife.

spinner dolphins at Fernando de Noronha archipelago, both in Brazil; June–Sept/Oct: southern right whales southern Santa Catarina Island. June–Dec: humpbacks in National Marine Park of Abrolhos in Brazil.
*Weather* Amazon–Orinoco hot, humid conditions; in southern Brazil, whale season is cold, windy, even from lookouts, often rough on the water.
*Types of tours* Half- and full-day tours, some extended multi-day expeditions; inflatables, sailboats, motorboats, canoes and river ferries; some watching from land.
*Tours available* Brazil: Manaus, Florianópolis, Caravelas; Colombian Amazon: Bogotá, Leticia, and Puerto Nariño; Peru: Iquitos.
*Special features* In Santa Catarina, you may witness rare cooperation between humans and dolphins. Some 200 bottlenose dolphins

reside inshore around the mouth of a large lagoon near the coastal city of Laguna. The dolphins come close to shore (except in June and July) for mullet fishing. For long periods groups of 25–30 dolphins help human fishers by driving the fish closer to shore and into the nets. The dolphins, of course, get some of the fish for themselves.

### Argentina

*When to visit* Mid-July–Nov, southern right whales at Península Valdés, Patagonia, best Aug–Oct; orcas year-round but catch sea lions on beaches mid-Feb to mid-Apr; Dec–Mar, Commerson's dolphins and Peale's dolphins near Puerto Deseado
*Weather* Mid-July–Nov: cold during right whale season, cool at sea even on best days for dolphin watching in Dec–Mar.

*Types of tours* Mainly extended multi-day expeditions, some day tours locally; inflatables, fishing boats, sport-fishing boats, sailboats, kayaks.
*Tours available* Buenos Aires; Chubut province: Puerto Pirámide, Puerto Madryn, Rawson, Trelew; Santa Cruz province: Puerto San Julian, Puerto Deseado.
*Special features* Several cetacean species are found only around the tip of southern South America. The best studied of these is Commerson's dolphin, a small black and white dolphin, which can be seen on dolphin-watch tours out of Puerto Deseado in the far south of Argentina. Because spring weather is poor in these far southern waters, the best viewing season is December to March.

# EUROPE AND AFRICA

**Commercial cetacean watching in Europe and Africa started in 1980, when a Gibraltar fisherman began offering boat tours to see three species of Mediterranean dolphins. By the mid-1980s, trips were being offered in France, Britain, Ireland and Portugal to see dolphins.**

### The industry spreads

As whale-watch tours began to flourish in Europe, interest in land-based watching of southern right whales was growing on the South African coast, but it wasn't until the end of the 1980s that whale and dolphin watching really took off there. In addition, substantial industries started up in Norway, Italy and the Canary Islands, followed closely by the Azores. Whale watching for sperm whales and various baleen whales out of Andenes, in northern Norway, is in many ways a model for successful ecotourism. Experienced naturalists, or nature guides, and scientists work on board whale-watch boats, and a museum and whale center are located in the town.

### Italy and the Azores

In Italy, guided fin whale tours out of Porto Sole and San Remo, near Genoa, have become popular. In the Azores, there is an amazing diversity of cetaceans and both land- and boat-based whale watching.

**The Canary Islands** The Canary Islands, off southern Morocco, have had the fastest growth in whale watching of anywhere in the world. Between 1991 and 1996, the number of people watching whales grew from fewer than 1,000 to an estimated 50,000 visitors a year taking trips on at least 46 registered boats, owned by some 31 companies.

### WATCHING AT MIDNIGHT

The newest and perhaps the most exciting area for whale watching in the world is Iceland, where whale watchers began visiting in numbers as recently as 1995. Tourists are now arriving from all over Europe, North America and even farther afield, to watch and photograph whales against a dramatic background of volcanoes, icefields—and the midnight sun.

This makes the Canary Islands one of the three largest whale-watching destinations in the world, along with southern New England and the St. Lawrence River. There are outstanding opportunities for observing local short-finned pilot whales and various dolphins. However, few operators carry naturalists on board, so make inquiries about who the responsible operators are.

**Fine whale watching** Apart from the Canary Islands, Europe and Africa have been responsible for some of the finest whale-watching tours. In South Africa and Ireland, in particular, well-developed walking tours have given participants a chance to see the whales during guided tours along the cliffs. From Italy, Greece, Croatia, France and some other countries people may sign up for 3–10 days to accompany scientists on high-quality tours that make significant contributions to the conservation of numerous species of cetaceans.

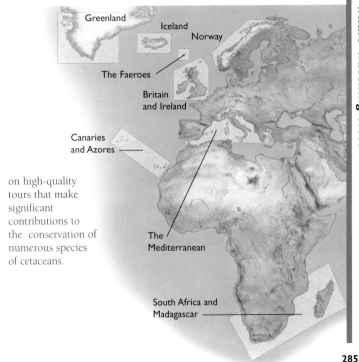

Greenland

Iceland

Norway

The Faeroes

Britain and Ireland

Canaries and Azores

The Mediterranean

South Africa and Madagascar

### Iceland

*When to visit*  May–Sept: several cetacean species (humpback whales more in early summer, orcas in late summer); best period June–Aug.

*Weather*  Cold on the water; rain and rough seas intermittent; snow is possible early and late in whale-watch season.

*Types of tours*  Half- and full-day tours, some extended multi-day expeditions; fishing boats and large tour boats.

*Tours available*  Húsavík, Höfn, Dalvík, Hauganes, Stykkishólmur, Keflavík, Grindavík, Ólafsvík, Arnarstapi.

*Special features*  In northeastern Iceland, near Húsavík, there is superb bird watching in the Lake Myvatn area. Species include some rare ducks. There is also regular volcanic activity nearby, which can be seen in hot, spluttering mudholes and a lunar landscape.

### Norway

*When to visit*  Late May–Sept in the Andenes area for sperm and other whales and dolphins; Oct to mid-Nov around Tysfjord for orcas.

*Weather*  Cold on the water late May–Sept in Andenes and Oct–Nov in Tysfjord; Tysfjord has very short days (few hours daylight by mid-Nov).

*Types of tours*  Half- and full-day tours, some extended multi-day expeditions; inflatables, sailboats and large boats.

*Tours available*  Andenes, Nyksund, Myre, Stø, Storjord.

*Special features*  In the Andenes area, on Bleiksoy Island, is one of Norway's better bird cliffs. Two-hour tours visit the colony, where puffins, kittiwakes, storm petrels, common guillemots, fulmars and numerous cormorants breed.

**FIN WHALE**
Although sperm whales are the main attraction in Norwegian waters, fin whales (right) are one of a wide range of other species that are often sighted there.

of Ilulissat (Jakobshavn) is the most active glacier in the Northern Hemisphere, which produces about 20 million tons (18 million tonnes) of ice every day. Greenland Tourism offers a range of nature, glacier, cultural and historical tours by helicopter, boat, kayak and dogsled.

### ICY ENVIRONMENT

For much of the year the waters around Iceland are littered with giant icebergs. Whale-watching tours are limited to the warmer months.

### Greenland and the Faeroe Islands

*When to visit* June–Aug: Greenland; Sept–Oct: whales common but weather can be poor; May–Oct Faeroes.
*Weather* Cold on the sea, rain and snow a possibility.

*Types of tours* Half- and full-day tours, some extended multi-day expeditions; kayaks, fishing boats, large touring boats.
*Tours available*
Greenland: Paamiut (Frederikshåb), Aasiaat, and Ilulissat (Jakobshavn) in Disko Bay, Ammassalik; the Faeroe Islands: Tórshavn, Sandur
*Special features* Just 28 miles (45 km) east

### COASTAL VISITOR

Blue whales nomally feed offshore, but may occasionally be seen close inshore off northeastern Iceland.

# EUROPE AND AFRICA continued

### Britain and Ireland

*When to visit* Year-round: dolphins but best seen May–Oct; Apr–Oct: minke whales in western and northern Scotland; June–Aug: prime whale- and dolphin-watching season.

*Weather* Cool to cold on the water; rain possible, even in summer, especially in western parts of Britain and in Ireland.

*Types of tours* Half- and full-day tours, extended multi-day expeditions; inflatables, sailboats and large whale-watch boats; some whale watching from ferries; land-based whale watching.

*Tours available* Britain: (England) Cornwall; (Wales) New Quay, Milford Haven; (Scotland) Dervaig (on the Isle of Mull), Mallaig, Oban, Gairloch, Cromarty, Inverness; Republic of Ireland: Carrigaholt, Dingle, Schull, Castlehaven, Kilbrittain, Clifden.

*Special features* Communities in Britain and Ireland have long had friendly relationships with solitary bottlenose dolphins.which were given names such as Freddy, Percy and Simo. The latest dolphin is Fungie, who moved into Dingle Harbour, County Kerry, Ireland, in the mid-1980s.

### The Mediterranean

*When to visit* June–Sept: best for most cetaceans, although they are present year-round; May–Oct: best for dolphins around Gibraltar, but

**FUNGIE TERRITORY**
Dingle Harbour, County Kerry, Ireland, is home to Fungie, a solitary bottlenose dolphin that seems to delight in entertaining human spectators.

Barcelona; Greece: Kalamos Island; Croatia: Veli Losinj.
*Special features* Few visitors to the Mediterranean realize that fin whales spend their summers just offshore in the Ligurian Sea, west of northern Italy.

### NORTHERN BOTTLENOSE
Scottish whalers used to call old northern bottlenose whale bulls "flatheads." Tens of thousands have been killed since then.

*Tours available* Italy: Porto Sole, San Remo, Imperia; France: Toulon; Gibraltar; Spain: Almería,

### NEAR GREECE
Sperm whales are among several species found off Greece, east of southern Italy, in summer.

tours also Nov–Jan.
*Weather* Sept: hot, dry, although sea breezes keep temperatures comfortable; May–Oct: can be cool with occasional rough seas; Nov–Apr: cool, sometimes cold at sea with rainstorms.
*Types of tours* Half- and full-day tours, extended multi-day expeditions; inflatables, sailboats, fishing boats:

### The Canaries and the Azores

*When to visit* Year-round Canaries: short-finned pilot whales, bottlenose, common and many other tropical dolphins, along with small, toothed whales. May–Oct Azores: sperm, other whales, but whales may also be seen before and after this period.

*Weather* Canaries: subtropical year-round with cool, refreshing winds; sometimes hot, sandy desert winds from Africa make whale sighting difficult, but there are usually 300 good whale-watching days per year; May–Oct Azores: seas windy, cool to cold.

*Types of tours* Half- and full-day tours, some extended multi-day expeditions; sailboats and large whale-watch boats.

*Tours available* Canary Islands: Los Cristianos and Puerto Colón, near Playa de las Americas, on Tenerife, Gomera, Lanzarote, Gran Canaria; Azores: Horta on Faial; Lajes on Pico.

*Special features* In the Azores, the "vigias," or lookout towers where whalers kept watch, have been restored by whale-watch companies. Many of them, especially on Pico and Faial, are open to visitors.

### South Africa and Madagascar

*When to visit* July–Nov: southern right whales in South Africa; July–Sept: humpback whales, and a chance to see mating behavior and calves in Madagascar; year-round bottlenose, Heaviside's and Indo-Pacific humpback dolphins.

*Weather* July–Nov in South Africa: weather mixed, with rain and strong winds alternating with moderate to high temperatures; July–Sept: humpback season in Madagascar, warm weather even at sea.

**OUT FROM TENERIFE**
Bottlenose dolphins can often be seen within an hour of leaving Tenerife in the warm, deep waters of the Canary Islands.

**IN AFRICAN SEAS**
In South African waters, Fraser's dolphins (left), which are often shy of boats in other areas, frequently ride the bow waves. On Madagascar's east coast, around the island of Nosy Boraha, humpback whales (below) return every year from July to September to mate and raise their young.

*Types of tours* Mainly land-based lookouts and tours; boat tours for dolphin watching in South Africa; small-boat and fishing-boat tours in Madagascar.

*Tours available* South Africa: Hermanus, Plettenberg Bay (various), Lambert's Bay; Madagascar: Andampanangoy.

*Special features* Many parks in South Africa and Madagascar are close to whale-watching sites. A South African wildlife area close to the whale-watching sites is the Cape of Good Hope Nature Reserve. There are also a number of easily accessible colonies of Magellanic penguins that are well worth visiting in the Cape Province region.

# ASIA

As Japan leads the way, whale watching, and especially dolphin watching, is catching on in fishing villages and beach resorts all over Asia. It is proving its worth as a source of income in this vast region, where many people depend on the sea for their livelihoods.

**Japan** In April 1988, the first Japanese whale-watching expedition departed from Tokyo for the Ogasawara Islands. This trip was so notable because Japan remains both a whaling nation and a consumer of whale meat. Since 1988, Japanese whale watching has flourished. Some 25 communities around the country now offer whale- and dolphin-watching tours. With a whale-watching season of only three months a year, the Ogasawara whale-watch industry provides half of the year's tourist income to the islands. That is almost half that of the most important industry—fishing. In some communities, the local government or fishing collective sponsors whale watching. In other areas, local fishers and dive operators have organized the whale-watch tours. Many Japanese travelers have experienced whale watching in Hawaii, Canada or Baja California, so it was perhaps inevitable that they would take ideas back to their own country. More than 60,000 people a year now take whale- and dolphin-watching tours in Japanese waters.

**Hong Kong** In Hong Kong, dolphin tours have already become popular. The tours are based on the resident pink Indo-Pacific hump-backed dolphins and finless porpoises that are seen in some of

---

**CONSERVATION PROBLEMS**

In Hong Kong, dolphin watching has alerted many people to the problems of conserving dolphins, which are being displaced from local waters by industry. In Japan and China, along with other countries in Asia, the hope is that cetacean watching will expand and become even more important as an economic, educational, scientific and conservation force.

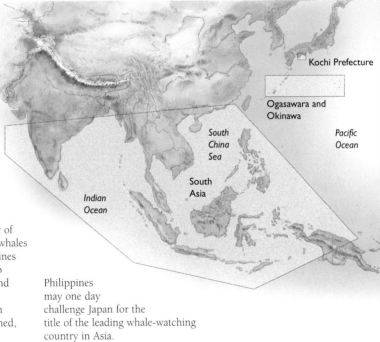

the most well-traveled waterways of the world.

## Other regions

In other parts of Asia, whale watching is still a developing industry. In Goa, India, small boats take beachgoers to meet tropical dolphins offshore. The same is true in Bali, Indonesia; off Phuket, Thailand; and off the east coast of Taiwan. Because of the wide diversity of species offered, from sperm whales to rare dolphins, the Philippines has the potential to appeal to discerning whale watchers and ecotourists. A number of educational and conservation programs have been established, and it is possible that the Philippines may one day challenge Japan for the title of the leading whale-watching country in Asia.

Kochi Prefecture

Ogasawara and Okinawa

South China Sea

Pacific Ocean

South Asia

Indian Ocean

293

## ASIA continued

### South Asia

*When to visit*  Year-round: dolphins throughout region, sperm whales off Sri Lanka; Feb–Apr: blue whales off Sri Lanka; Apr–June: best for Philippines.

*Weather*  Hot, but conditions vary across this vast region; main obstacles are prevailing winds that make whale watching in exposed areas difficult.

*Types of tours*  Half- and full-day tours, some extended multi-day expeditions; small boats, sailboats, canoes, outrigger boats and motor cruisers; some land-based whale watching. Visitors arriving during storm and monsoon seasons should pay attention to local weather advice.

*Tours available*  Hong Kong; India: Goa; Thailand: Phuket; Indonesia: Lovina Beach on Bali; Philippines: Tagbilaran on Bohol.

*Special features*  The survival of local whale populations depends partly on the ability of local communities to make a living from being able to show visitors "their" local wildlife.

**TROPICAL SPECIES**
Numerous tropical dolphin species inhabit the waters offshore from the beaches of Goa, India.

## Japan: Ogasawara and Okinawa

*When to visit* Feb–Apr: humpbacks winter on mating and calving grounds around Ogasawara and Okinawa and the Kerama Islands; year-round: various dolphins.

*Weather* Warm to hot during the season, but often windy and cool at sea.

*Types of tours* Half-day tours; inflatables, diving and fishing boats; some whale watching

**SPINNERS**

In the Tañon Strait of the Philippines, many tropical dolphins, such as these spinner dolphins, may be seen.

from ferries.

*Tours available* Chichi-jima and Haha-jima in the Ogasawara Islands; Zamami and Tokashiki in the Kerama Islands; Naha on Okinawa.

*Special features* Japanese scientists on whale-watching boats in Ogasawara and the Keramas have complied a photo-identification catalog of more than 6,000 individual humpback whales.

## Japan: Kochi Prefecture

*When to visit* Mar–Oct (best May–Sept): Bryde's whales off Ogata, Saga and other communities in Kochi Prefecture; year-round: dolphins in most locales, plus short-finned pilot whales and sperm whales off Cape Muroto, near Muroto, but best Mar–Dec.

*Weather* Oct: varies from cool to warm at sea; Nov–Feb: cool to cold at sea; typhoon season Aug to early Oct.

*Types of tours* Half- and full-day tours; fishing boats; some watching from ferries.

*Tours available* Ogata, Saga, Shimonokae, Tosa-shimizu, Kochi City, Cape Muroto.

*Special features* The whales watched at Otaga, which is the most popular whale-watching community in Japan, are predominantly Bryde's whales. Photo-identification studies show that at least 15 Bryde's whales are present in Tosa Bay. From March to October, they come in close to shore to feed.

# AUSTRALIA AND OCEANIA

**Whale watching throughout Australia and Oceania has mostly developed during the 1990s. Australia and New Zealand have led the way, aided by well-developed domestic travel industries that help support whale watching, attracting visitors from far and wide.**

**Migrating humpbacks** In Australia, humpback and southern right whale watching was mostly land-based until 1987, when boat-based tours, operating out of Hervey Bay, Queensland, gained in popularity. Along with members of many communities near the eastern and western coasts of Australia, watchers avidly follow the annual migrations of humpback whales.

**Southern rights** Australia also offers outstanding destinations for viewing migrating southern right whales. In Warrnambool, Victoria, since the early 1980s, the southern right whale nursery at Logan's Beach has attracted thousands

---

**BENEFITS OF TOURISM**

Whale watching throughout the South Pacific is boosting tourism, and probably also helping to encourage whale conservation. Some tours are associated with research work or, occasionally, diving tours. Tonga has taken the lead with humpback tours to meet mothers and calves that are wintering near the islands.

---

of visitors every year. Some adventurous tourists trek to the Head of the Great Australian Bight or the Bunda Cliffs, along the Eyre Highway, for some of the most spectacular cliffside whale watching in the world.

**Monkey Mia** At Monkey Mia, in Western Australia, bottlenose dolphins have enjoyed a friendly relationship with humans for many years. Thousands of people visit every year, wading in the shallow water, where dolphins come to interact with their land-based neighbors. Several other dolphin populations are found in inshore waters around Australia, and these have awakened the keen interest of researchers and whale watchers alike.

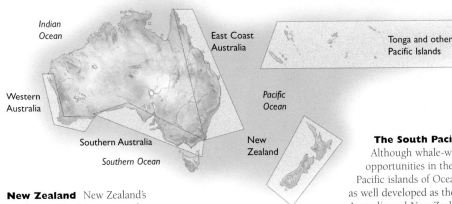

Indian
Ocean

East Coast
Australia

Tonga and other
Pacific Islands

Western
Australia

Pacific
Ocean

Southern Australia

New
Zealand

*Southern Ocean*

### The South Pacific

Although whale-watching opportunities in the South Pacific islands of Oceania are not as well developed as those in Australia and New Zealand, they are expanding. Tonga leads the field, but other places—including Tahiti, Niue, Moorea, Fiji, New Caledonia and Western Samoa—also have nascent whale-watching industries.

**New Zealand**  New Zealand's whale watching began around the same time as Australia's, but has since taken off in different directions and with a flavor all its own. Whales spotted around New Zealand are largely toothed whale species that are resident rather than migratory. Sperm whale watching at Kaikoura, New Zealand's premier watching site, has helped create one of the world's most charming communities dedicated to whale watching. Elsewhere around New Zealand, rare dolphins lend a special magic to the watching—the Hector's dolphin is found only in New Zealand waters. Dusky dolphins, also seen in a number of other Southern Ocean locations, are still most frequently spotted here.

### East Coast Australia

*When to visit*  Humpback whales: Queensland, including Hervey Bay, Aug–Nov; New South Wales, including Wollongong, late May–mid-July, late Sept–Nov, and Eden, June–July, Oct–Nov. Dolphins: year-round.

*Weather*  Queensland coast: warm to hot on humpback breeding grounds; New South Wales: cool to cold on water.

*Types of tours*  Half- and full-day tours, some extended multi-day expeditions; inflatables, sailboats, diving boats and large whale-watch boats; land-based whale watching also good.

*Tours available*  Queensland: Airlie Beach, Bundaberg, Hervey Bay, Tangalooma; New South Wales: Byron Bay, Coffs Harbour, Eden, Fairy Meadow, Wollongong.

*Special features*  The town of Eden, about 300 miles (485 km) south of Sydney, on Twofold Bay, offers a combination of historical whaling

### WINTER BREEDING GROUNDS

Humpback whales, as well as various dolphins, can be seen in the pristine waters between the Great Barrier Reef, which stretches almost the entire length of the Queensland coastline, and the mainland. From Airlie Beach, near the town of Bundaberg, tours depart to see humpback whales on their winter breeding grounds in the waters surrounding the Whitsunday Islands.

interest and whale-watching tours. These tours can catch migrating humpbacks during their northerly migration in June and July and their return south in October to November. Because Twofold Bay is near the far southeastern corner of Australia, it is both the first and last land point that the humpbacks pass on their long journey to and from Antarctica. Visitors are also likely to see bottlenose dolphins near Twofold Bay and, sometimes, southern right and blue whales. They may also catch sight of Australian fur seals.

### FAVORITE VANTAGE POINT

Fraser Island, off the coast of southern Queensland near Hervey Bay, is a favorite land base for watching migrating humpbacks, which can often be seen playing close to the shore along Platypus Bay, on the northeastern side of the island. This wonderful island, the world's largest sand island, also boasts many other natural attractions. These include spectacular sand dune formations, evocative sand cliffs, numerous lakes, rain forests and heathlands covered in wildflowers.

### AQUATIC PERFORMER

Whale watchers at many places along the east coast of Australia are able to observe huge humpbacks going through their paces, rolling over and over in the wake the boat, as if to show off the extensive whiteness of their bellies, pectoral fins and flukes, and creating great cascades of froth and foam. Southern Hemisphere humpbacks are known to be whiter on the underside than their northern counterparts, although both are considered the same species.

### Southern Australia

*When to visit*  Year-round: bottlenose dolphins at the Head of Bight, South Australia, and Port Phillip Bay, Victoria (summer best at south end of bay); May–Oct: southern right whales at the Head of Bight and other bays along the South Australia coast; mid-June–Oct: southern right whales at Head of Bight and Victor Harbor,

SA, and Logan's Beach, Vic.
*Weather*  Cool to cold on the water, but can be warm from sheltered lookouts.
*Types of tours*  Largely land-based whale watching, some organized as multi-day expeditions, but most are informal day trips; some half- and full-day boat tours, inflatables and small boats out of Port Phillip Bay.

*Tours available*  South Australia: Ceduna, Victor Harbor; Victoria: Moorabbin, Logan's Beach.
*Special features*  Visitors to Australia's southeastern coast can watch dolphins. One accessible population lives in Port Phillip Bay, Victoria. More than 100 bottlenose dolphins living here have been photo-identified since 1990.

### Western Australia

*When to visit*  Year-round bottlenose dolphins at Monkey Mia (Apr–Oct, dolphins approach swimmers most often, with less

### TALL FINS
Although the southern right whale is by far the most commonly seen whale along the coast of southern Australia, the distinctive tall dorsal fins of orcas (left) are also frequently seen in this region. Orcas also often come into Victoria's Port Phillip Bay.

**IDYLLIC WHALE WATCHING**
Few communities have become so captivated and identified with whales and dolphins as Kaikoura—a small town at the foot of snow-capped mountains on the east coast of New Zealand's South Island. Sperm whales are the main attraction.

Albany, Denham, Monkey Mia (land-based watching).
*Special features* Monkey Mia, 505 miles (810 km) north of Perth, attracts 100,000 visitors a year. They come primarily to see and to interact with a group of six bottlenose dolphins which swim close to shore almost every day. These dolphins approach people who wade into the water, nudging the humans' legs and allowing themselves to be touched. Although the composition of this group of dolphins has changed from time to time, the number has remained more or less constant.

frequent sightings Nov–Mar); May–Oct southern right whales (Aug–Nov is prime for Albany area); Sept–Nov humpbacks in Perth area (July–Sept in northern part of Western Australia).
*Weather* Generally cool on the sea for boat-based whale watching; shore-based dolphin and whale watching can be warm or even hot in summer months, particularly at Monkey Mia.
*Types of tours* Half- and full-day tours, some extended multi-day expeditions; inflatables, sailboats and large boats; land-based whale watching.
*Tours available* Perth, South Perth, Hillary's Harbour, Fremantle, Geraldton, Exmouth, Carnarvon,

### New Zealand

*When to visit* Year-round: sperm whales, Hector's, common and bottlenose dolphins; Oct–May: dusky dolphins close to shore (esp. Kaikoura).

*Weather* Cool (summer) to cold (winter) on the sea, at Kaikoura, on the South Island and southern North Island; cool (winter) to warm (summer) on the sea from Bay of Plenty to Bay of Islands, on the North Island.

*Types of tours* Half- and full-day tours, extended multi-day expeditions; inflatables, sailboats, motorboats, large whale-watch boats; some whale watching from ferries, helicopters and fixed-wing aircraft.

*Tours available* South Island: Kaikoura, Akaroa, Picton, Te Anau; North Island: Paihia, Tauranga, and Whakatane.

*Special features* Visitors to Kaikoura will see sperm whales. They also have the rare chance to see the Hector's dolphin—a small, attractive dolphin that is found only in New Zealand waters.

### A GROWING INDUSTRY

The beautiful islands of the South Pacific are becoming increasingly important as starting points for whale-watching tours. A wide range of whales and dolphins can be observed and studied in these tropical waters.

### STUDIES IN FIJI
In 1995 photo-identification research began on a small pod of spinner dolphins living near the Fijian islands of Tavarua and Namotu, which are better known as destinations for surfers.

*Tours available* Tonga: Vava'u; Fiji: Nadi; French Polynesia: Moorea; New Caledonia: Noumea.

*Special features* No matter what island you visit, don't miss the coral reef diving. The greatest biological diversity in the South Pacific is invariably underwater. If you can't scuba dive, try snorkeling. Fiji, "the soft coral capital of the world," has year-round diving only 10–15 minutes by boat from most resorts. Some of the species to be seen include hundreds of hard and soft corals, sea fans and sea sponges. There is also a wide variety of often colorful fish and other marine life. Be aware, however, that coral is alive and fragile—only travel with ecologically sound operators.

### APTLY NAMED
The aptly named melon-headed whale, one of the smallest animals to be called a "whale," lives in tropical and subtropical waters and feeds on squid and fish.

## Tonga and other Pacific Islands
*When to visit* July–Nov: humpback whales in Tonga; year-round: tropical dolphins in all locations, but Apr–Oct best for weather.
*Weather* Hot during dry season, Apr–Oct; sun averages 6–8 hours a day, even in wet season.
*Types of tours* Half- and full-day tours, some extended multi-day expeditions; inflatables, sailboats, kayaks and diving boats.

# THE POLES

Before whaling began, the Arctic and Antarctic regions, in summer, held the greatest density of whales on Earth. But almost 400 years of whaling in the Arctic and just over a half-century in the Antarctic resulted in the severe depletion of many species. Even now, many whales in these regions are struggling to survive.

**Late starters**  When the first cruise ship visited the Antarctic Peninsula in 1957, whale watching was unheard of. By the 1980s, however, it had become a key feature of organised tours there. Since whale-watching trips in the Arctic began in the early 1980s, the industry has steadily expanded, despite difficulties with access to many areas.

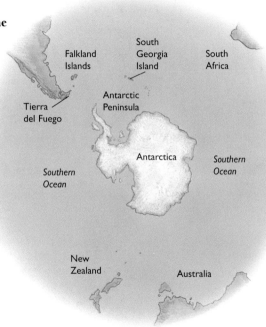

Falkland Islands

South Georgia Island

South Africa

Tierra del Fuego

Antarctic Peninsula

Antarctica

*Southern Ocean*

*Southern Ocean*

New Zealand

Australia

**The Arctic** Tours are now available to the far north of Canada, Greenland, Norway and Russia to observe bowheads, narwhals and belugas—cetacean species that are found only in Arctic regions.

**The Antarctic** Antarctic cruises offer the chance to see minke, humpback, blue, fin and sei whales, as well as sperm whales, beaked whales, orcas and hourglass dolphins.

### CASUALTIES

Arctic whaling began in 1607 off Svalbard, north of Norway. The bowhead whale was the first Arctic casualty, with many other species following. In the first half of the twentieth century, until the 1960s, hundreds of thousands of whales were killed in the Antarctic. Blue whales there are still endangered.

305

### The Arctic

*When to visit*  June–Aug for most of the Arctic; Aug best for belugas and polar bears in Churchill.
*Weather*  Cold on water throughout the Arctic, snow possible; Churchill, warm temperatures by day, often dipping to freezing at night.
*Types of tours*  Half- and full-day tours, some extended multi-day expeditions; inflatables, sailboats and large whale-watch boats.
*Tours available*  Canada: Churchill; Greenland: Uummannaq; Norway: Sveagruva on Svalbard.
*Special features*  Perhaps the most accessible subarctic location is Churchill, on Hudson Bay, northern Manitoba, Canada. Churchill is accessible by jet or 40-hour passenger train from Winnipeg. Although it is considerably south of the Arctic Circle, belugas come in close to the mouth of the Churchill River, swimming some miles upriver from June through August.

### Antarctica

*When to visit*  Late Nov–Mar: baleen whales—humpback, minke, fin—feed around Antarctica, along with orcas and hourglass dolphins. The window for sailing to Antarctica is only 3–4 months.
*Weather*  Cold—take winter gear even in Antarctic summer; cruise

### AT BOTH POLES

Fin whales can be seen in subarctic and Antarctic waters, where they were abundant prior to whaling. In the St. Lawrence River, they often travel in pods of 5 to 10, swimming and feeding together in a tight group.

### HEADING INLAND

Belugas, which are confined to Arctic and subarctic waters, have been known to swim hundreds of mile up rivers in Canada, Russia and northern Europe.

as well as visits to Antarctic research stations. The cruises are offered by various companies based in the United States, Canada, Britain, Germany, Australia and New Zealand. There are a few air tours to Antarctica, but these are not recommended as a means of whale watching.

ships offer shelter, but dress warmly to see whales close up from deck or inflatable boats launched from the ship.

*Types of tours* Extended multi-day expeditions.

*Tours available* Check local travel agent. Some cruise ships carry inflatables for close viewing.

*Special features* The only way for most people to get to Antarctica and watch whales is aboard a large cruise ship. These trips are not exclusively whale-watching tours, but extended cruises that include sightings of birds, seals, icebergs, penguins and cetaceans,

### TOURIST ATTRACTIONS

Numerous species of penguins live in Antarctica and provide a major attraction for visitors to the region.

# CLASSIFICATION TABLE

Whales, dolphins and porpoises—the order Cetacea—are elusive creatures and can be extremely difficult to study. Consequently, our understanding of their classification is changing all the time, especially with recent advances in genetic research. There is some contention as to how many species exist: new ones are still being discovered and there are constant discussions about whether others should be split into two or three different species. Therefore, while the classification and scientific names used here are accepted by the majority of cetologists (biologists who study cetaceans), some remain controversial, and future studies will, almost inevitably, lead to changes. The most frequently used common name is listed first; alternatives are in brackets.

## ORDER CETACEA

**SUBORDER MYSTICETI** — **BALEEN WHALES**

**Family Balaenidae** — **Right Whales**

*Balaena mysticetus* — bowhead whale (Greenland right whale)

*Eubalaena glacialis* — northern right whale (black right whale, Biscayan right whale & North Atlantic right whale)

*Eubalaena australis* — southern right whale (black right whale)

**Family Neobalaenidae** — **Pygmy Right Whale**

*Caperea marginata* — pygmy right whale

**Family Eschrichtiidae** — **Gray Whale**

*Eschrichtius robustus* — gray whale (Pacific gray whale & California gray whale)

**Family Balaenopteridae** — **Rorquals**

*Balaenoptera musculus* — blue whale

*Balaenoptera physalus* — fin whale (finback & finner)

*Balaenoptera borealis* — sei whale

*Balaenoptera edeni* — Bryde's whale (tropical whale)

*Balaenoptera acutorostrata* — minke whale (little piked whale)

*Megaptera novaeangliae* — humpback whale

**SUBORDER ODONTOCETI**     **TOOTHED WHALES**

**Family Physeteridae**     **Sperm Whale**
*Physeter macrocephalus*     sperm whale (cachalot)

**Family Kogiidae**     **Pygmy and Dwarf Sperm Whales**
*Kogia breviceps*     pygmy sperm whale
*Kogia simus*     dwarf sperm whale

**Family Monodontidae**     **White Whales**
*Monodon monoceros*     narwhal
*Delphinapterus leucas*     beluga (belukha, white whale & sea canary)

**Family Ziphiidae**     **Beaked Whales**
*Tasmacetus shepherdi*     Shepherd's beaked whale (Tasman beaked whale)
*Berardius arnuxii*     Arnoux's beaked whale (southern four-toothed whale)
*Berardius bairdii*     Baird's beaked whale (northern four-toothed whale)
*Mesoplodon pacificus*     Longman's beaked whale (Indo-Pacific beaked whale)
*Mesoplodon bidens*     Sowerby's beaked whale (North Sea beaked whale)

*Mesoplodon densirostris*     Blainville's beaked whale (dense-beaked whale)
*Mesoplodon europaeus*     Gervais' beaked whale (Antillean beaked whale)
*Mesoplodon layardii*     strap-toothed whale
*Mesoplodon hectori*     Hector's beaked whale
*Mesoplodon grayi*     Gray's beaked whale (scamperdown whale)
*Mesoplodon stejnegeri*     Stejneger's beaked whale (Bering Sea beaked whale)
*Mesoplodon bowdoini*     Andrew's beaked whale (splay-toothed beaked whale)
*Mesoplodon mirus*     True's beaked whale (wonderful beaked whale)

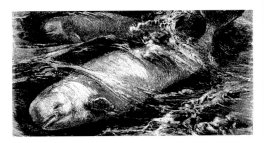

| | |
|---|---|
| *Mesoplodon ginkgodens* | ginkgo-toothed beaked whale |
| *Mesoplodon carlhubbsi* | Hubb's beaked whale |
| *Mesoplodon peruvianus* | Peruvian beaked whale (lesser beaked whale & pygmy beaked whale) |
| *Mesoplodon bahamondi* | Bahamonde's beaked whale |
| *Mesoplodon species "A"* | Unidentified beaked whale |
| *Ziphius cavirostris* | Cuvier's beaked whale (goose-beaked whale) |
| *Hyperoodon ampullatus* | northern bottlenose whale |
| *Hyperoodon planifrons* | southern bottlenose whale |

| **Family Delphinidae** | **Dolphins and Other Small, Toothed Whales** |
|---|---|
| *Peponocephala electra* | melon-headed whale |
| *Feresa attenuata* | pygmy killer whale |
| *Pseudorca crassidens* | false killer whale (pseudorca) |
| *Orcinus orca* | orca (killer whale) |
| *Globicephala melas* | long-finned pilot whale (pothead, blackfish) |
| *Globicephala macrorhynchus* | short-finned pilot whale |
| *Orcaella brevirostris* | Irrawaddy dolphin |
| *Steno bredanensis* | rough-toothed dolphin |

| | |
|---|---|
| *Sotalia fluviatilis* | tucuxi (estuarine dolphin) |
| *Sousa chinensis* | Indo-Pacific humpback dolphin (Chinese white dolphin) |
| *Sousa teuszii* | Atlantic humpback dolphin |
| *Lagenorhynchus albirostris* | white-beaked dolphin (squidhound) |
| *Lagenorhynchus acutus* | Atlantic white-sided dolphin |
| *Lagenorhynchus obscurus* | dusky dolphin |
| *Lagenorhynchus obliquidens* | Pacific white-sided dolphin |
| *Lagenorhynchus cruciger* | hourglass dolphin |
| *Lagenorhynchus australis* | Peale's dolphin |
| *Lagenodelphis hosei* | Fraser's dolphin |
| *Delphinus delphis* | short-beaked common dolphin (saddleback dolphin & common porpoise) |
| *Delphinus capensis* | long-beaked common dolphin (saddleback dolphin & common porpoise) |
| *Tursiops truncatus* | bottlenose dolphin |
| *Grampus griseus* | Risso's dolphin (grampus) |
| *Stenella attenuata* | pantropical spotted dolphin |
| *Stenella clymene* | short-snouted spinner dolphin (clymene dolphin) |
| *Stenella frontalis* | Atlantic spotted dolphin |

| | |
|---|---|
| *Stenella longirostris* | long-snouted spinner dolphin (spinner) |
| *Stenella coeruleoalba* | striped dolphin (streaker) |
| *Lissodelphis peronii* | southern right whale dolphin |
| *Lissodelphis borealis* | northern right whale dolphin |
| *Cephalorhynchus heavisidii* | Heaviside's dolphin |
| *Cephalorhynchus eutropia* | black dolphin (Chilean dolphin) |
| *Cephalorhynchus hectori* | Hector's dolphin (New Zealand dolphin) |
| *Cephalorhynchus commersonii* | Commerson's dolphin |

**Family Phocoenidae** — **Porpoises**

| | |
|---|---|
| *Phocoena phocoena* | harbor porpoise (common porpoise) |
| *Phocoena spinipinnis* | Burmeister's porpoise |
| *Phocoena sinus* | vaquita (cochito & Gulf of California porpoise) |
| *Australophaena dioptrica* | spectacled porpoise |
| *Phocoenoides dalli* | Dall's porpoise (spray porpoise) |
| *Neophocaena phocaenoides* | finless porpoise (black finless porpoise & black porpoise) |

**Family Platanistidae** — **Ganges and Indus River Dolphins**

| | |
|---|---|
| *Platanista gangetica* | Ganges river dolphin (Ganges susu, gangetic dolphin & blind dolphin) |
| *Platanista minor* | Indus river dolphin (Indus susu & bhulan) |

**Family Iniidae** — **Amazon River Dolphin**

| | |
|---|---|
| *Inia geoffrensis* | Amazon river dolphin (bouto, boto & pink dolphin) |

**Family Pontoporiidae** — **Baiji & Franciscana**

| | |
|---|---|
| *Lipotes vexillifer* | baiji (Yangtze river dolphin, Chinese river dolphin, beiji, whitefin dolphin & whiteflag dolphin) |
| *Pontoporia blainvillei* | franciscana (La Plata dolphin) |

# INDEX

Entries in *italics* indicate illustrations and photos.

# Z

*Ziphius cavirostris* 156-7

## ACKNOWLEDGMENTS

Weldon Owen would like to thank the following people: Sarah Anderson, Lisa Boehm, Trudie Craig, Peta Gorman, Michael Hann, Janet Healey, Aliza Pinczewski, Puddingburn Publishing Services (index)

TEXT Dr. Lawrence G. Barnes, Dr. M. M. Bryden, Mark Carwardine, Peter Corkeron, Dr. William H., Dawbin, Hugh Edwards, Dr. R. Ewan Fordyce, Linda Gibson, Peter Gill, Sir Richard Harrison, Erich Hoyt, Dr. Margaret Klinowska, Dr. Robert J. Morris, Marty Snyderman, Dr. Ruth Thompson, Dr. Kaiya Zhou

ILLUSTRATIONS Kenn Backhaus, Alistair Barnard, Martin Camm, Christer Eriksson, Ray Grinaway, Gino Hasler, Robert Hynes, David Kirshner, Frank Knight, Stan Lamond, Tony Pyrzakowski, Rod Scott, Roger Swainston, Ann Winterbotham

PHOTOGRAPHS Ad-Libitum/Stuart Bowey, Apple Computer Australia Pty Ltd, Auscape/Jean-Paul Ferrero, The Bridgeman Art Library, Corel Corporation, Peter Gill, Debra Glasgow, P. Hodda, International Whaling Commission, Mary Evans Picture Library, Paddy Pallin, Photo Essentials, Weldon Owen, Weldon Owen/Oliver Strewe.

CONSULTANT EDITOR Peter Gill, Researcher, lecturer and writer, Sydney, New South Wales, Australia.